The Language Teaching Matrix

CAMBRIDGE LANGUAGE TEACHING LIBRARY
A series of authoritative books on subjects of central importance for all language teachers

The Language Teaching Matrix

Jack C. Richards

City Polytechnic of Hong Kong

The right of the
University of Cambridge
to print and publish
all kinds of books
was granted by law
in 1534
The University has printed
and published continuously
since 1584

Cambridge University Press
Cambridge
New York   Port Chester
Melbourne   Sydney

Published by the Press Syndicate of the University of Cambridge
The Pitt Building, Trumpington Street, Cambridge CB2 1RP
40 West 20th Street, New York, NY 10011, USA
10 Stamford Road, Oakleigh, Melbourne 3166, Australia

First published 1990
Second printing 1990

Printed in the United States of America

Library of Congress Cataloging-in-Publication Data
Richards, Jack C.
The language teaching matrix / Jack C. Richards.
p.   cm. – (Cambridge language teaching library)
Includes biographical references.
ISBN 0-521-38408-7 (hardback) – ISBN 0-521-38794-9 (paperback)
1. Language and languages – Study and teaching.   I. Title.
II. Series.
P51.R48   1990
418'.007–dc20   89-37999
                                                         CIP

British Library Cataloguing in Publication Data
Richards, J. C. (Jack Croft)
The language teaching matrix – (Cambridge language teaching library).
1. Foreign languages. Teaching
I. Title
418'.007

ISBN 0-521-38408-7 hardback
ISBN 0-521-38794-9 paperback

Chapter 2 is a revised version of an article that originally appeared in
Prospect 3, 1 (September 1987).

Chapter 3 is a revised version of "Designing Instructional Materials
for Teaching Listening Comprehension," RELC Anthology Series, Materials for Language Learning and Teaching. Cambridge University
Press is grateful to RELC for permission to publish this article.

Chapter 5 is a revised version of an article that originally appeared in
Prospect 4, 2 (January 1989).

Contents

Preface

The Language Teaching Matrix is designed to serve as a textbook in courses on language teaching methodology and teacher preparation, and as a source book for courses on language curriculum design, materials development, and teaching practice. The "matrix" in the title is a metaphor for an interactive and multidimensional view of language teaching; for in this book effective language teaching is seen to result from interactions among the curriculum, teachers, students, methodology, and instructional materials. In particular, three factors are singled out as central to effective teaching: the curriculum, methodology, and instructional materials.

This is not a book of prescriptions, where teaching is approached in terms of *methods,* or *products* that offer teachers predetermined models to follow. Rather, teaching is approached as a dynamic *process.* Teaching depends upon the application of appropriate theory, the development of careful instructional designs and strategies, and the study of what actually happens in the classroom. Because these ingredients will change according to the teaching context, effective teaching is continually evolving throughout one's teaching career. Discussion questions and tasks at the end of each chapter will aid teachers in their personal journeys toward effective teaching.

Each chapter in the book takes a central issue in language teaching and examines its position within the language teaching matrix – that is, its role and position within the network of factors that have to be considered. Chapter 1 presents an overview of curriculum development processes and suggests that an effective second language program depends upon careful information gathering, planning, development, implementation, monitoring, and evaluation. Chapter 2 contrasts two approaches to conceptualizing the nature of methodology in language teaching. One is the familiar methods-based approach to teaching. This is seen to be a "top-down" approach because it involves selecting a method, then making teachers and learners match the method. The other is a "bottom-up" approach; it involves exploring the nature of effective teaching and learning, and discovering the strategies used by successful teachers and learners in the classroom. This chapter hence seeks to draw attention away from methods and to address the more interesting question of how successful teachers and learners achieve their results.

The next four chapters of the book focus on the teaching of listening, speaking, reading, and writing. Each skill is discussed from a different perspective.

Chapter 3 looks at a key issue in the teaching of listening comprehension: the design of suitable instructional materials. It is argued that teaching materials should recognize the difference between two kinds of listening processes, referred to as top-down and bottom-up processing. In addition, differences between interactional and transactional purposes for listening are discussed. These distinctions are then used as a framework for designing listening exercises.

In the next chapter, teaching conversation is approached through an examination of the nature of casual conversation and conversational fluency. Two approaches are compared – an indirect approach, which teaches conversation through the use of interactive tasks, and a direct approach, which focuses on the processes and strategies involved in casual conversational interaction. The need to monitor classroom activities to determine their effectiveness in promoting conversation skills is emphasized.

In Chapter 5 a case study is presented of an effective reading teacher. From interviews and video recordings of the teacher's class, an attempt is made to understand how the teacher approaches his teaching and the kinds of planning and decision making that the teacher employs. In Chapter 6 approaches to the teaching of writing are considered. The importance of an adequate theory of writing is stressed, and product- and process-based approaches to teaching writing are compared. Implications for the roles of learners, the teacher, and instructional activities are discussed.

Chapter 7 discusses ways in which teachers can explore the nature of their own classroom practices and improve the effectiveness of their teaching through self-monitoring. Three approaches to self-monitoring are elaborated: personal reflection through journal or diary accounts of teaching, self-reports based on focused reports of lessons, and audio or video recordings of lessons. Practical suggestions are given on what teachers can look for in their own lessons, procedures for carrying out self-monitoring, and how to use the information obtained.

In Chapter 8 approaches to developing programs for students of limited English proficiency are considered. Traditionally language proficiency has been the main focus of such programs. The goal has been to develop minority students' language skills to a level where they can cope with the demands of regular classroom instruction. It is suggested that this approach is inadequate, and that an effective program must address three crucial dimensions of classroom learning, referred to as the interactional dimension (the ability to understand and use the social rules of classroom discourse), the instructional task dimension (the ability to understand the nature of learning in mainstream classrooms), and the cognitive dimension (the ability to understand and assimilate concepts and information in different content areas).

The book concludes with a short chapter offering reflections on some of the key points of the book. The primary goal of *The Language Teaching Matrix* is to engage teachers and teachers-in-training, as well as teacher educators, in the investigation of classroom teaching and learning. In order to facilitate this and to assist instructors using the book, each chapter concludes with a set of discussion questions and practical activities. These serve to link the information in each chapter with practical issues in curriculum development, methodology, classroom observation, and materials design.

This book resulted from graduate courses I taught as a faculty member of the Department of English as a Second Language at the University of Hawaii, from 1981 to 1988. Discussions with students and colleagues helped clarify my understanding of many of the issues discussed here. For ongoing support, advice, and encouragement while the book was being written, I am particularly grateful to my former colleagues Richard Day, Richard Schmidt, and Martha Pennington. Others whose advice has always been both constructive and supportive include particularly Chris Candlin, Fred Genesee, David Nunan, and Tom Scovel. Lastly, special thanks are due to Ellen Shaw at Cambridge University Press, whose guidance and encouragement helped shape the book into a more readable and coherent form; to Barbara Curialle Gerr, who saw the book through production; and to Sandra Graham, whose skillful copy editing helped remove many a circumlocutious thought and infelicitous phrase – though not this one!

The Language Teaching Matrix

1 Curriculum development in second language teaching

Second language teaching is often viewed from a very narrow perspective – that of the teaching act. Consequently much of the literature on second language teaching deals with teaching methods or with the design and use of instructional materials. If students aren't learning it is assumed to be the fault of the method, the materials, or the teacher. Yet the success of a language program involves far more than the mere act of teaching. As with any successful educational program, a number of levels of planning, development, and implementation are involved. Goals and objectives for the program have to be developed as well as syllabuses and instructional materials. Instructional strategies have to be determined, teachers selected and trained, and tests and assessment procedures chosen. Once the program is in operation, procedures are needed to enable the program to be monitored and its effects on learners and learning evaluated. In order to plan for effective second language teaching, a comprehensive view is needed of the nature and process of language program development. Providing such a view is the goal of this chapter, in which issues and practices in language curriculum development are reviewed and their contribution to effective language teaching assessed.

Language curriculum development, like other areas of curriculum activity, is concerned with principles and procedures for the planning, delivery, management, and assessment of teaching and learning. Curriculum development processes in language teaching comprise needs analysis, goal setting, syllabus design, methodology, and testing and evaluation.

Needs analysis

Needs assessment refers to an array of procedures for identifying and validating needs, and establishing priorities among them. (Pratt 1980:79)

In language curriculum development, needs analysis serves the purposes of:

1. providing a mechanism for obtaining a wider range of input into the content, design, and implementation of a language program through

1

involving such people as learners, teachers, administrators, and employers in the planning process

2. identifying general or specific language needs that can be addressed in developing goals, objectives, and content for a language program
3. providing data that can serve as the basis for reviewing and evaluating an existing program.

In language teaching, the impact of needs analysis has been greatest in the area of special-purposes program design, and a considerable literature now exists on the role of needs assessment in English for specific purposes (ESP) (Robinson 1980). But needs analysis is also fundamental to the planning of general language courses.

Parameters, sources, and procedures

Needs analysis may focus on either the general parameters of a language program or on the specific communicative needs of language learners. The first approach may be referred to as *situation analysis,* and involves focusing on the following kinds of questions:

Who are the learners?
What are the learners' goals and expectations?
What learning styles do the learners prefer?
How proficient are the teachers in the target language?
Who are the teachers?
What training and experience do the teachers have?
What teaching approach do they favor?
What do teachers expect of the program?
What is the administrative context of the program?
What constraints (e.g., time, budget, resources) are present?
What kinds of tests and assessment measures are needed?

The second approach, *communicative needs analysis* (Munby 1978), is concerned with gathering information about the learners' communicative needs in the target language, and involves questions such as these:

In what settings will the learners use the target language?
What role relationships are involved?
Which language modalities are involved (e.g., reading, writing, listening, speaking)?
What types of communicative events and speech acts are involved?
What level of proficiency is required?

Answers to these questions help determine the type of language skills and level of language proficiency the program should aim to deliver. An example of a questionnaire in the domain of situation analysis is given in Appendix 1, and one in the domain of communicative needs analysis in Appendix 2.

Determining needs is not an exact science, however, since it involves both quantitative and qualitative approaches, requires the use of a variety of formal and informal data-gathering procedures, and seeks to identify or quantify needs that may be by nature imprecise. Needs statements thus represent judgments by the needs analyst as to what should be analyzed, the means to be used, and the meaning and significance of the data collected. Methods employed in gathering data vary according to setting and may involve participant observation, interviews, question-naires, content analysis of job descriptions and job advertisements, tests, role play, and analysis of communication breakdowns (Roberts 1980; Schroder 1981).

Needs-analysis procedures generate a considerable amount of data, including information about the context of the language program, the learners, the teachers, and the administrative factors that affect the pro-gram. This information is then used in planning the program itself. Let us examine some of the key processes involved in more detail.

Goals and objectives

Curriculum goals are general statements of the intended outcomes of a language program, and represent what the curriculum planners believe to be desirable and attainable program aims based on the constraints revealed in the needs analysis. Goals can be used as a basis for developing more specific descriptions of the intended outcomes of the program (the program objectives). Goal statements refer to elements of the program that are actually going to be addressed by instruction. For example, a needs analysis might reveal that a group of learners had unfavorable attitudes toward the proposed language program. A goal statement re-flecting this might be:

Students will develop favorable attitudes toward the program.

However, while this goal might represent a sincere wish on the part of teachers, it should appear as a program goal only if it is to be addressed concretely in the program.

From goals to objectives

In language teaching, a number of different ways of stating program objectives are commonly employed, including behavioral, skills-based, content-based, and proficiency-based objectives.

BEHAVIORAL OBJECTIVES

The most familiar way to state objectives is in terms of behavior. Mager (1962) specified three essential characteristics of behavioral objectives:

1. They must unambiguously describe the behavior to be performed;
2. They must describe the conditions under which the performance will be expected to occur;
3. They must state a standard of acceptable performance (the criterion).

Findlay and Nathan (1980) give examples of behavioral objectives in "competency-based" language programs. Sample objectives for a survival language course include:

Given an oral request, the learner will say his/her name, address and telephone number to a native speaker of English and spell his/her name, street and city so that an interviewer may write down the data with 100% accuracy.

Given oral directions for a 4-step physical action, the learner will follow the directions with 100% accuracy.

Sample objectives for an ESP course for clerical workers are:

Given a letter with 10 proofreading marks for changes, the learner will rewrite the letter with 90% accuracy in 10 minutes.

Given the first and last names of 10 persons, five with Spanish surnames and five with English surnames from a local telephone directory, the learner will locate the names and write down the telephone numbers in 5 minutes with 90% accuracy. (Findlay and Nathan 1980: 226)

Four justifications are commonly made to support the use of behavioral objectives in curriculum planning:

1. They help teachers to clarify their goals.
2. They facilitate instruction by highlighting the skills and subskills underlying different instructional content.
3. They make the evaluation process easier.
4. They provide a form of accountability.

A criticism that is often made, however, is that representing language teaching goals in terms of behavioral objectives is impractical, as well as undesirable. Some learning goals cannot readily be stated in terms of behavioral changes expected in students. In such cases, it is preferable to focus on the classroom tasks and learning activities that learners should engage in, and the intrinsic worth and value of these experiences for their own sake, without specifying precise learning outcomes. This is sometimes referred to as a process-based approach (Stenhouse 1975).

Behavioral objectives also tend to deal only with aspects of second language proficiency that can be represented as "competencies" and hence tend to trivialize the nature of second language acquisition.

SKILLS-BASED OBJECTIVES

A common way of stating objectives in language programs is to specify "microskills," or processes that account for fluency in such specific "macroskill" areas as reading, writing, listening, and speaking. In specifying microskills, the curriculum planner tries to describe the competencies that account for functional ability in a given skill but are "independent of specific settings or situations" (Krahnke 1987: 49). For example, Nuttall (1983: 146) presents objectives for an intensive reading program in the following form:

After completing the reading course, the student will:
a) Use skimming when appropriate to ensure that he reads only what is relevant, to help subsequent comprehension.
b) Make use of non-text information (especially diagrams etc.) to supplement the text and increase understanding.
c) Read in different ways according to his purpose and the type of text.
d) Not worry if he does not understand every word, except when complete accuracy is important.
e) Recognize that a good writer chooses his words carefully and would have meant something different if he had chosen A rather than B. (An advanced reader will be able to explain the difference.)
f) Make use of the reference system, discourse markers, etc., to help himself unravel the meaning of difficult passages.
g) Be aware that a sentence with the same signification may have a different value in different contexts, and be able to identify the value.
h) Be able to make use of the rhetorical organization of the text help him interpret a complex message.
i) Be aware that a writer does not express everything he means, and be able to make inferences as required.
j) Be aware that his own expectations influence his interpretation and recognize those occasions when the writer's assumptions differ from his own.
k) Be aware, when necessary, that he has not understood the text, and be able to locate the source of misunderstanding and tackle it.
l) Respond fully to the text in whatever way is appropriate.

Richards (1985a: 199) lists among the microskills needed for academic listening the ability to

1. identify the purpose and scope of a lecture
2. identify and follow the topic of a lecture

3. identify relationships among units within discourse (e.g., major ideas, generalizations, hypotheses, supporting ideas, examples)
4. identify the role of discourse markers in signaling the structure of a lecture
5. infer relationships (e.g., cause, effect, conclusion)
6. recognize key lexical items related to a topic
7. deduce meanings of words from context.

Krahnke (1987) discusses the advantages and disadvantages of a skills-based approach. Relevance to students' needs is a key advantage, whereas the potential ambiguity and subjectivity of skills taxonomies are disadvantages.

CONTENT-BASED OBJECTIVES

Many language programs specify objectives in relation to content. For example, the Council of Europe's Threshold Level English (Van Ek and Alexander 1980: 29) includes objectives related to fourteen topic areas. Under the topic "House and Home," for example, the following are among the specifications given:

Learners should be able to discuss where and under what conditions they live, specifically:

types of accommodation	describe the type of house, flat etc in which they live themselves, as well as those in the neighborhood, and seek similar information from others
accommodation, rooms	describe their own accommodation, house, flat, etc and the rooms in it, and seek similar information from others
furniture, bedclothes	mention and inquire about the availability of the most essential pieces of furniture and bedclothes
rent	state, rent and/or purchase price of their own accommodation and inquire about that of other houses, flats, etc

Lists of functions, often related to specific situations or settings, are also employed as objectives in language programs. For example, a syllabus guide for vocational English in industry lists "core needs" in the following form (MacPherson and Smith 1979):

To ask:
    someone to lend you something
    someone to pass something that's out of reach
To ask for:
    change in deductions
    change in holiday dates

change in shift
help from workmates when the job is too much for one person

It is clear that in using skills taxonomies and content-based descriptions as objectives, the distinction between "objectives" in the sense proposed by Mager and "syllabus" – that is, between goals and content – has been blurred.

PROFICIENCY SCALES

A related development in language curriculum development is the use of proficiency scales. Program objectives may specify a level of proficiency, such as "survival English," or "Level 3 on the Foreign Service Oral Proficiency Scale." An example of the use of proficiency-based objectives in large-scale language program design is the Australian Adult Migrant Education On-Arrival Program, a program for immigrants (Ingram 1982).

In order to ensure that a language program is coherent and systematically moves learners along the path towards that level of proficiency they require, some overall perspective of the development path is required. This need resulted...in the development of the Australian Second Language Proficiency Ratings (ASLRP). The ASLRP defines levels of second language proficiency at nine (potentially twelve) points along the path from zero to native-like proficiency. The definitions provide detailed descriptions of language behaviour in all four macroskills and allow the syllabus developer to perceive how a course at any level fits into the total pattern of proficiency development. (Ingram 1982: 66)

Likewise instruments such as the Foreign Service Institute Oral Interview (a scale that contains five levels of oral proficiency supplemented by ratings for accent, grammar, vocabulary, and fluency) can be used not only to assess proficiency for diagnostic or placement purposes but also to establish levels of proficiency as program objectives. The American Council on the Teaching of Foreign Languages (ACTFL) in 1982 published Provisional Proficiency Guidelines, which are "a series of descriptions of proficiency levels for speaking, listening, reading, writing, and culture in a foreign language. These guidelines represent a graduated sequence of steps that can be used to structure a foreign-language program" (Liskin-Gasparro 1984: 11). However, Ingram and others have stressed that proficiency descriptions complement rather than replace the use of program objectives since, particularly at the lower levels, they tend to resemble profiles of incompetence and hence are hardly suitable as statements of objectives (Brindley 1983: 39). It has also been observed that there is little relevant empirical data available to develop valid statements of proficiency levels across skill areas, an issue that has proved

7

problematic with the ACTFL proficiency scales (Lee and Musumeci 1988).

No matter what approach to stating goals and objectives is used, all language programs operate with explicit or implicit objectives. Where the program fails to make objectives explicit, teachers and learners have to infer them from the syllabus, materials, or classroom activities. Teachers may hence regard objectives merely as instructional goals (e.g., "to develop learners' confidence in speaking"), as course descriptions (e.g., "to concentrate on listening skills"), or as descriptions of the material they intend to cover (e.g., "to cover Chapter 3 of *Strategies*") (Brindley 1984). Without clear statements of goals and objectives, questions of content, methodology, and evaluation cannot be systematically addressed.

Syllabus design

In standard models of curriculum processes, curriculum planners progress systematically from needs assessment, to goals and objectives, to specification of the instructional content of the program. Taba's model of curriculum processes (1962: 12) consists of:

Step 1: Diagnosis of needs
Step 2: Formulation of objectives
Step 3: Selection of content
Step 4: Organization of content
Step 5: Selection of learning experiences
Step 6: Organization of learning experiences
Step 7: Determination of what to evaluate and means to evaluate

In language teaching, Steps 3 and 4 are usually known as *syllabus design*. Syllabus design (the product of which is usually referred to as a *syllabus* in British usage and a *curriculum* in American usage) is concerned with the choice and sequencing of instructional content. If the Taba model were followed, the procedures for developing a syllabus would involve examining instructional objectives and arranging them by priorities, and then determining what kind of content was required to attain the objectives.

In reality, in language teaching the syllabus has traditionally been the starting point in planning a language program, rather than an activity that occurs midway in the process. The concept of a language syllabus has been fundamental in the development of language teaching practices in the twentieth century. In the work of such British language teaching specialists as Harold Palmer, Michael West, and A. S. Hornby, and such American specialists as Charles Fries and Robert Lado, questions con-

8

cerning the linguistic content of a language program were considered primary and a necessary basis for planning a language program. This reflects the fact that many applied linguists were trained as linguists, rather than as educational planners. Hence from the 1920s through to the present, debate over the most appropriate form for syllabuses in language teaching has continued. A properly constructed and planned syllabus is believed to *assure* successful learning, since it represents a linguistically and psycholinguistically optimal introduction to the target language. Syllabus design theory has consequently been one of the most active branches of applied linguistics in recent years (e.g., Wilkins 1976; Shaw 1977; Yalden 1983; Krahnke 1987; Nunan 1988) – to the astonishment perhaps of those with a broader educational view of curriculum issues.

Conceptions of the nature of a syllabus are closely related to the view of language and second language learning that the curriculum designers subscribe to. Under the impact of grammar-based views of the nature of language, language syllabuses were traditionally expressed in terms of grammar, sentence patterns, and vocabulary. As a result of the more recent movement toward communicative theories of language and language learning, syllabuses have tended to be expressed more in communicative terms. The following kinds of syllabuses (or variants and combinations of them) are commonly found in current English as a second language (ESL) courses and materials, particularly those dealing with speaking and listening.

1. Structural (organized primarily around grammar and sentence patterns)
2. Functional (organized around communicative functions, such as identifying, reporting, correcting, describing)
3. Notional (organized around conceptual categories, such as duration, quantity, location)
4. Topical (organized around themes or topics, such as health, food, clothing)
5. Situational (organized around speech settings and the transactions associated with them, such as shopping, at the bank, at the supermarket)
6. Skills (organized around skills, such as listening for gist, listening for specific information, listening for inferences)
7. Task or activity-based (organized around activities, such as drawing maps, following directions, following instructions)

Despite the extensive literature on syllabus design in recent years, there is little empirical evidence to warrant commitment to any particular approach to syllabus development. In practice, a combination of approaches is often used, since many would agree with Johnson (1981: 34):

A syllabus is essentially a job specification, and as such it should set out clearly and precisely what is to be done, and the standards or criteria to be met by those who do it. If seen in this light, arguments as to the relative merits of notional, situational, or topic based syllabuses, etc. are no more sensible than arguments as to whether the specifications in a construction contract should cover the foundations, or the steel framework or the concrete or the glass or the interior design etc. The obvious answer is that all of these must be covered.

In addition, it should be emphasized that the form in which a syllabus is presented reflects the intended users and uses of the syllabus. Is the syllabus primarily a guide for materials writers, or are classroom teachers expected to teach from it? Is the syllabus a document teachers will consult, and if so, what do they expect to find in it? Will learners be tested on the content of the syllabus, or are teachers free to adapt and supplement it? What teaching skills and teaching styles do the teachers have who will be using the syllabus? The effect of different answers to these kinds of questions is seen when syllabuses are compared.

Appendix 3, for example, is taken from the *Malaysian Communicational Syllabus* (1975), a syllabus for the teaching of English in upper-secondary school. The syllabus specifies activities and tasks rather than notions, functions, grammar, or vocabulary, as well as the level at which tasks are to be accomplished. Procedures suggested for classroom use include various kinds of communication tasks, role plays, and simulations, and the syllabus provides sample situations as a guide to the teacher. The syllabus reflects the philosophical assumptions of the syllabus planners: a commitment to communicative language teaching and to a needs-based approach to program content. At the same time the syllabus assumes that teachers have a high degree of proficiency in English and are able to adapt and plan materials and classroom activities around the syllabus. The syllabus was also intended as a guide for textbook writers, who were expected to write materials that exemplified the principles of the syllabus.

The syllabus example in Appendix 4 is very different in form and approach. This is part of a tutor's kit intended for volunteers working with Vietnamese refugees in Britain. In this case the syllabus is planned around topics and content, and a great deal more linguistic specification is given. This reflects the fact that the users of this syllabus were not expected to have the same high degree of training and experience as the teachers using the Malaysian syllabus.

Appendix 5 is from a syllabus for refugees in the United States who need survival-level skills to enter the job market. The philosophy of the syllabus planners is evident in the "competencies" specified, which provide clear guidelines for both teaching and testing. The syllabus is planned around topics, and competencies are listed for each topic area. Teachers are expected to teach to the syllabus and to test students in and out of the program based on the learners' mastery of the content of the syllabus.

Methodology

It is not until the goals, objectives, and content of a language program have been determined that decisions about methodology can be taken up in detail. The focus of this phase of program development is on the kind of instruction that will be required to achieve the goals of the program. From the perspective of curriculum development, questions of methodology do not center on the choice of a "method." (See Chapter 2 for a detailed critique of this approach to teaching.) Appropriate teaching methodology is not predetermined; nor can it be imposed on teachers and learners. Rather, it evolves out of the dynamics of the teaching process itself (see Chapters 2 and 5). This does not mean, however, that effective teaching cannot be planned for and conceptualized in advance.

Methodology can be characterized as the activities, tasks, and learning experiences selected by the teacher in order to achieve learning, and how these are used within the teaching/learning process. These activities are justified according to the objectives the teacher has set out to accomplish and the content he or she has set out to teach. They also relate to the philosophy of the program, to the view of language and language learning that the program embodies, and to the roles of teachers, learners, and instructional materials in the program. Since the assumptions underlying methodology are not necessarily shared by teachers, administrators, and learners, it is a useful exercise for all who are involved in a language program to clarify their assumptions about the kind of teaching and learning the program will try to exemplify. This can be done through teacher preparation activities that examine attitudes, beliefs, and practices concerning five central issues:

1. the approach or philosophy underlying the program
2. the role of teachers in the program
3. the role of the learners
4. the kinds of learning activities, tasks, and experiences that will be used in the program
5. the role and design of instructional materials.

The approach or philosophy

First, assumptions about the nature of language and language learning need to be clarified. What view of the subject matter or content of the course (e.g., listening to lectures, reading for study purposes, conversation skills for social survival) does the program reflect? For example, is reading viewed as primarily a "top-down" or "bottom-up" process (see Chapter 4)? What does listening comprehension involve and what skills does it depend upon? How is conversation understood and what are its most important components? In order to answer questions like these, teachers and curriculum planners need to find ways of clarifying and sharing their perceptions and beliefs in order to reach an understanding of the very skill they are setting out to teach. If different viewpoints are not resolved, teachers may set about their teaching in ways that seem incorrect or puzzling to each other or to a program supervisor.

Closely related to the teachers' understanding of the nature of language and the specific aspects of language proficiency that the program sets out to teach is their understanding of how proficiency in reading, writing, listening, and speaking is achieved. What beliefs do teachers have about how people acquire conversational skills, learn to write effectively, or gain a better mastery of the phonology or grammar of the target language? What theory of second language learning do the teachers subscribe to, and how divergent or relevant to the particular program are the beliefs or assumptions they hold? Opportunities for clarification of these questions should be planned for during the curriculum development process.

The role of the teacher

Teaching is usually regarded as something that teachers do in order to bring about changes in learners. A central component of methodology is how teachers view their role in this process. What kinds of teaching style do they regard as desirable? What kinds of teacher–learner interactions do they favor? The following are among the kinds of roles teachers may see for themselves in the classroom:

monitor of student learning
motivator
organizer and controller of pupil behavior
provider of accurate language models
counselor and friend
needs analyst
materials developer
evaluator

The roles teachers adopt form the basis for teachers' decisions on how the program's activities, techniques, and learning experiences can best be used to bring about learning. In thinking about these kinds of issues, teachers can better understand the assumptions that guide their own teaching. Willing (1985) suggests a number of values-classification and other kinds of exercises that enable teachers to explore these issues. For example, teachers may discuss such questions as:

1. Suppose a total stranger walked in and observed one of your classes. What aspects of your teaching style would give that person clues as to your basic personality?
2. What aspects of your teaching style might mislead that same person about your true personality?
3. Who does best in your classes? How would you describe a typical "excellent learner" for the sort of teaching you do?
4. Have you ever gone through a major change of teaching style?

(Willing 1985: 14)

Procedures that teachers can use to monitor and examine their own teaching are given in Chapter 7.

The role of the learners

How do those involved in the program view the role of learners in the learning process? How are learners expected to learn within the program? Are they viewed as the passive recipients of an educational technology that is imposed on them, or are they viewed as having active input into the learning process? To what extent will learners be consulted concerning the kinds of learning and learning activities they will undertake? What will characterize a good approach to learning from the point of view of both teachers and learners? Is there any conflict between this and the learners' view of their role in learning and their approach to learning? The role of the learners will therefore relate to:

approaches to learning
attitudes to learning
preferred learning styles and strategies
preferred learning activities
patterns of learner-to-learner interaction
patterns of teacher-to-learner interaction
degree of control learners exercise over their own learning
how learners characterize effective teaching
how learners characterize effective learning

Information obtained during needs analysis will be useful in thinking about these issues. When such information is not available in advance, it should be sought as the program is being implemented (i.e., as part of formative evaluation, discussed later in this chapter).

Learning activities, tasks, and experiences

Teaching consists of the activities, tasks, and learning experiences selected to help bring about learning, and how these are used in the classroom. What principal kinds of activities, tasks, and learning experiences will the program make use of and what criteria will be used for selecting them? How much weight will be assigned to each activity type per lesson/unit, and what configurations of teacher and learners will activities involve? A conversation course, for example, may include the following activities:

pair work or group work (learner to learner)
practice with the text (teacher to learner)
free conversation (teacher to learners / learner to learner)
dialogue work (learner to learner)
pronunciation exercises (teacher to learner)

These activities are selected on the basis of the kinds of conversational interaction and the opportunities for conversational practice they bring about. A writing course, on the other hand, may be organized around activities such as the following:

brainstorming (learner to group)
quickwriting (learner to self)
group writing (learner to group)
peer feedback sessions (learner to group)
blackboard writing (teacher to group)
free composition activities (learner to self)
analysis of models of good writing (teacher to group)

Activities are selected according to the opportunities they provide for developing composing skills (planning, drafting, revising) as well as for gaining control of the mechanics of writing.

Instructional materials

Methodology also depends upon the role of instructional materials in the program. The following kinds of questions will have to be asked at this point:

1. Will materials provide the primary source of language input for the learners or are they merely viewed as supplementing input provided by the teacher?

2. Will materials be adopted, adapted, or specially prepared for the program? Which of these options is best matched to the financial resources available and to the skills/abilities of teachers in the program?
3. If existing materials are going to be used (e.g., commercially published textbooks), what kind of preparation will teachers need in order to use them effectively?
4. If materials are to be specially written for the program, who will be involved in preparing them and under what circumstances?
5. Will adequate provisions be made for development, testing, and revision of the materials?

Good instructional materials are an important part of the process of instruction. They set out to teach through the process of

defining instructional objectives
setting learning tasks or activities to attain the objectives
informing learners of what tasks they have to perform
providing guidance in how to perform tasks
providing practice in performing tasks
providing feedback on performance
enhancing retention of the skills the learner acquired through performing the task.

At the same time, effective instructional materials in language teaching have the following characteristics:

They are based on theoretically sound learning principles.
They arouse and maintain the learners' interest and attention.
They are appropriate to the learners' needs and background.
They provide examples of how language is used.
They provide meaningful activities for learners.
They provide opportunities for communicative and authentic language use.

Attention to these kinds of issues is an essential aspect of the design of effective instructional materials.

Testing and evaluation

Testing occupies a central role in curriculum development, since it is often a component of both needs assessment and evaluation, and has consequences for the design and delivery of instruction as well as for the administration of the program itself. A large number of decisions made in the course of designing and implementing a language program are hence dependent on the use of tests. Traditionally four different kinds of tests have been distinguished in the literature on language testing according to the purposes for which they are typically used. *Proficiency tests* are tests that measure how well a learner can use a language relative to a specific purpose before a course of instruction, such as the TOEFL (Test of English as a Foreign Language), which is used to measure the English language proficiency of foreign students who wish to study in the United States. Proficiency tests are usually general in nature and not linked to a specific course of instruction. *Placement tests* are used to place students at an appropriate level within a language program. Although the same kinds of test items may be used in both a proficiency test and a placement test, proficiency tests are generally designed for a specific program or language course. *Achievement tests* measure how much of a language someone has learned in a particular course of study or program of instruction. They thus aim to measure gains in proficiency that result from the program itself, and can consequently be used to monitor the effectiveness of teaching, of the materials, or of the curriculum itself. *Diagnostic tests* aim to diagnose students' particular learning problems; for example, a diagnostic pronunciation test can be used to find out which aspects of English phonology a student is having difficulty with.

In recent years a further distinction has been made between norm-referenced and criterion-referenced tests. A *criterion-referenced* test is

a test which measures a student's performance according to a particular standard or criterion which has been agreed upon. The student must reach this level of performance to pass the test, and a student's score is therefore interpreted with reference to the criterion score, rather than to the scores of other students. (Richards, Platt, and Weber 1985)

This is contrasted with a *norm-referenced test,* which is

a test ... designed to measure how the performance of a particular student or group of students compares with the performance of another student or group of students whose scores are given as the norm. A student's score is therefore interpreted with reference to the scores of other students or groups of students, rather than to an agreed criterion score. (Richards et al. 1985)

A criterion-referenced approach to testing is often thought to be more appropriate to the proficiency-based view of language teaching increasingly being advocated in current discussions of language teaching, since tests should reveal whether students have developed the specific skills and proficiencies identified in the program objectives, rather than show how students' performances compare to each other. The test designer's goal, particularly for placement and achievement tests, is hence to develop tests that directly measure the kinds of language proficiencies described in the program objectives (see Dick and Carey 1985).

Evaluation is concerned with gathering data on the dynamics, effectiveness, acceptability, and efficiency of a program to facilitate decision making (Popham 1975; Jarvis and Adams 1979).

Evaluation is the determination of the worth of a thing. It includes obtaining information for use in judging the worth of a program, product, procedure or objective, or the potential utility of alternative approaches designed to attain specified objectives. (Worthen and Sanders 1973: 19)

The relatively short life span of most language teaching methods and the absence of a systematic approach to language program development in many institutions where English is taught are largely attributable to the fact that adequate allowance is not made for evaluation procedures in the planning process.

The primary focus of evaluation is to determine whether the goals and objectives of a language program are being attained – that is, whether the program is effective. When a decision must be made as to whether to adopt one of two possible program options geared to the same objectives, a secondary focus is on the relative effectiveness of the program. In addition, evaluation may be concerned with *how* a program works: that is, with how teachers and learners and materials interact in classrooms, and how teachers and learners perceive the program's goals, materials, and learning experiences. Evaluation differs from educational research in that even though it shares many of the procedures of educational research (tests, assessment, observation), information obtained from evaluation procedures is used to improve educational practices rather than simply describe them (Popham 1975).

Summative versus formative evaluation

A widely used distinction is between evaluation carried out at the completion of a course or program in order to measure how effective it was in attaining its goals (*summative evaluation*) and evaluation carried out during the development and implementation of a program, in order to modify and revise aspects of the program or the materials and to ensure the efficiency of the program (*formative evaluation*).

Summative evaluation may be used to support decisions about the continuation or modification of the program and typically involves the use of criterion-referenced or other achievement tests based on the program objectives. Typically differences between pretest and posttest scores are used as evidence of program effectiveness. Most institutions lack the resources necessary to measure a program's effectiveness through a true experimental design, using control or comparison groups. As Pratt notes,

There is adequate guidance in the literature as to how to control such factors as differences in student aptitude between two classes, but little as to how to control teacher differences in instruction; even the imposition of detailed lesson plans does not guarantee equivalent teaching. Finally, to compare the efficiency of two programs, they must be aiming at the same results and evaluated by tests equally appropriate to both curricula. (Pratt 1980: 421).

Other measures of a program's effectiveness are also available, however, such as interviews with graduates and dropouts from the program, interviews with employers and others who have contact with the learners after completion of the program, as well as interviews with teachers (Pratt 1980). Summative evaluation may be concerned with gathering data about a program over a period of years, which will ultimately be used to make decisions about the future of the program.

Formative evaluation addresses the efficiency and acceptability of the program, and frequently involves subjective and informal data (obtained, for example, from questionnaires or observation). Bachman suggests that the following processes are involved in formative evaluation:

The process of formative evaluation parallels that of program development, and comprises two types of activity: the internal assessment of what the program is supposed to be, and the gathering and interpretation of external information during field testing... Given a particular objective set, one aspect of internal assessment is to evaluate these objectives themselves. Is the rationale for each objective cogent? Are there undesired consequences associated with achieving certain objectives?... Another aspect of internal assessment is content-based review. Are the materials accurate? Do they constitute an appropriate range, in both difficulty and interest, vis-à-vis the learner?... Once the developer is satisfied, on the basis of the internal assessment, that the program incorporates the intended objectives and processes, he or she must then determine how it can most effectively produce the intended outcomes. This typically involves field testing. (Bachman 1981: 110–11)

Formative evaluation thus addresses such criteria as the appropriateness of the program's objectives; the degree of preparation of teachers; teachers' competence in the classroom; the usefulness of the syllabus, text, and materials; the effectiveness of scheduling and organization; the selection and use of test instruments. Pfannkuche proposes a comprehensive model that is characterized by a focus on the attainment of goals: "A certain set of learning goals and objectives are identified, and an assessment is made as to how well these goals are being met during the course of instruction" (Omaggio et al. 1979:254). This model involves the following processes:

1. Identify a set of program goals and objectives to be evaluated;...
2. Identify program factors relevant to the attainment of these objectives;...
3. For each factor in Step 2, develop a set of criteria that would indicate that the objectives are being successfully attained...
4. Design appropriate instruments to assess each factor according to the criteria outlined...

5. Collect the data that is needed.
6. Compare data with desired results...
7. Match or discrepancy?...
8. Prepare evaluation report...

(Omaggio et al. 1979: 254–63)

Pfannkuche emphasizes that such a comprehensive approach to formative evaluation can be realized only if one or two aspects of the language program are evaluated at a time; thus the total picture emerges over a period of several years.

Procedures used in conducting formative evaluation are varied. Bachman emphasizes that "although the most useful information is of an informal and subjective nature, this is not to say, however, that it cannot be systematic" (1981: 115). Evaluation of the program's objectives may involve the use of needs-analysis procedures; analysis of program characteristics may make use of checklists; in-class observation may provide data on the efficiency of the program and the use of equipment and materials; data on the processes actually used in teaching a class may be used to determine the degree of fit between the philosophy underlying a methodology and the classroom processes that result from it (Long 1983a); data on the acceptability and difficulty of materials may involve questionnaires to teachers and learners; enrollment and attrition figures for a program may be used as evidence of student attitudes about the program; interviews with students and teachers may identify weaknesses in content, sequencing, and materials; analysis of test results may be used to identify whether the content and methodology are consistent with the curriculum and appropriate to the objectives and the learners.

Although evaluation is discussed here as the final phase in the cycle of curriculum processes, evaluation processes apply to all phases of curriculum development, and formative evaluation procedures in particular have to be developed at the same time that objectives, syllabuses, learning content, and activities are being planned. Hence a curriculum can be viewed as a retrospective account of how an educational program was developed. For, as Stenhouse observes, "A curriculum, like the recipe for a dish, is first imagined as a possibility, then the subject of an experiment. The recipe offered publicly is in a sense a report on an experiment" (1975: 4).

Implications

The following dimensions of language curriculum development have been examined:

1. Needs analysis (situation analysis, communicative needs analysis)
2. Goals and objectives (behavioral objectives, skills-based objectives, content-based objectives, proficiency scales)
3. Syllabus design (syllabus types)
4. Methodology (approach or philosophy, role of the teacher, role of the learners, learning activities and tasks, instructional materials)
5. Testing and evaluation (proficiency tests, placement tests, achievement tests, diagnostic tests, summative evaluation, formative evaluation)

It has been stressed that effective language teaching programs are dependent upon systematic data gathering, planning, and development within a context that is shaped and influenced by learner, teacher, school, and societal factors. Each of these factors must be considered and addressed in educational program design. In an optimum program, design, content, instructional, learner, and teacher considerations are taken into account, as well as the broader questions that relate to the various levels of decision making. Potential conflicts are hence identified and system stability is aimed for. In moving toward a more cooperative perspective it is productive for participants at the different levels of educational decision making to have a more global view of the process of curriculum planning and of the various participants involved. In this way potential obstacles to successful design and implementation can be anticipated.

In Rodgers and Richards (1987) a practical approach to bringing this about is illustrated through the use of a Program Planning Profile (see Figure 1.1).[1] This consists of a problem-solving and group-discussion exercise for administrators, curriculum planners, and teachers that focuses on the different categories of considerations in curriculum design discussed here. These considerations are arranged under four categories: knowledge factors, learner factors, instructional factors, and administrative factors (Rodgers 1986). The profile is a device to stimulate group discussion, evaluation, and problem solving.

Curriculum development is typically a group planning process, and group planning plays an important part in almost all curriculum development projects that have been analyzed (e.g., see Schaffarzick and Hampson 1975). Central questions in this process concern how group educational planning can be most effective, how planning groups can be constituted and operate, and in particular, what factors planning groups should direct their attention to.

The factors proposed in the Program Planning Profile are ones that have emerged as worthy of early consideration from twenty years of curriculum design experiences of the staff of the Curriculum Research and Development Group at the University of Hawaii. The factor inven-

1 The rest of this chapter is adapted from Rodgers and Richards (1987).

tory has been revised several times and will undoubtedly be revised again. At this point, the factor inventory is intended to be more than suggestive but less than comprehensive.

The scales are organized so that low-difficulty factors are on the left and high-difficulty factors on the right. For example, if a proposed program's *subject area* (Factor 1) is already highly familiar to educators and the community (e.g., reading), the assessment would suggest "low difficulty" loading on this factor. If subject matter is highly unfamiliar (e.g., discourse analysis), assessment would indicate "high-difficulty" loading on this factor.

In use, each member of a planning group is given a profile sheet. The proposed educational program is described by the team leader and substantive questions are entertained. Each of the factor scales is "read" and briefly discussed to ensure a more or less common interpretation of the factor. Each of the participants then privately provides an assessment indicating which of the four points on the scale best represents the current status of that factor and marks the scale accordingly. The exercise leader may want to "pulse" this so that participants consider each factor equally and complete this phase of the exercise together. Participants then divide into subgroups of about four or five, each group containing a mix of people with different sorts of educational affiliations. The groups then discuss each factor (or a subset of factors) and comment on their individual assessments. Afterward a group secretary records assessment on a clean profile sheet. Consensus and disagreement are both important to note. The group then reconvenes as a whole, and secretaries report the results of the subgroup discussions.

The group can then make several kinds of assessments and determinations. For example:

1. How "difficult" does the project look as a whole? (Do assessments bias to the left/low-difficulty or to the right/high-difficulty end?)
2. What "high-difficulty" factors are most susceptible to manipulation, which could make them less difficult?
3. What factors will be most critical in the likely success or nonsuccess of the project?
4. When considerable disagreement exists as to assessment rating, why is this so? Would more data/discussion help?
5. Which factors contain the greatest unknowns? Could/should more information be gathered on these factors?
6. Do representatives with the same affiliations assess factors similarly? What are the implications for intergroup/intragroup communication and cooperation?

The following examples clarify the kinds of application that can be made from deliberation on the Profile.

Knowledge factors

1. Subject area	Familiar			Unfamiliar
	1	2	3	4
2. Knowledge base	Defined			Undefined
	1	2	3	4
3. Knowledge structure	Simple			Complex
	1	2	3	4
4. Relevant materials	Available			Unavailable
	1	2	3	4
5. Knowledge outcomes	Facts			Values
	1	2	3	4

Learner factors

6. Group size	Limited			General
	1	2	3	4
7. Homogeneity	Homogeneous		Heterogeneous	
	1	2	3	4
8. Teachability	Easy to teach		Hard to teach	
	1	2	3	4
9. Motivation	Aspiring		Non-aspiring	
	1	2	3	4
10. Attainment expectations	Basic		Sophisticated	
	1	2	3	4

Instructional factors

11. Curriculum design	Simple			Complex
	1	2	3	4
12. Educational plan	Well-researched		Intuitive	
	1	2	3	4

Figure 1.1   Program Planning Profile (from Rodgers and Richards 1987: 36–7)

Case A: A national communicative curriculum is proposed to replace a grammar/literature upper-secondary syllabus in an EFL situation. The planning group notes that communicative approaches are unfamiliar to teachers (Factor 1), locally relevant materials are unavailable (Factor 4),

13. Instructional media	Technically simple			Technically complex
	1	2	3	4
14. Teacher retraining possibilities	Extensive			None
	1	2	3	4
15. Target schools (system)	Coherent			Disjoint
	1	2	3	4
16. Target schools (problems)	Known/Simple		Unknown/Profound	
	1	2	3	4
17. Competing programs	None			Many
	1	2	3	4

Administrative factors

18. Change effort (breadth)	Local			International
	1	2	3	4
19. Change effort (depth)	Partial			Complete
	1	2	3	4
20. Development time	Extensive			Limited
	1	2	3	4
21. Development team	Experienced		Inexperienced	
	1	2	3	4
22. Agency reputation	Excellent		Poor/Unknown	
	1	2	3	4
23. Agency leverage	Great			Limited
	1	2	3	4
24. Development resources	Large			Small
	1	2	3	4

and time and resources for development for teacher retraining are highly limited (Factors 14, 20, 24). Deliberation suggests that because these and a number of other factors are weighted toward the high difficult end of the factor scales, a modest change in subject matter should be attempted initially. Using the principle of least change, a program built around communicative pair practice of exercise types familiar to and favored by teachers and maintenance of a literature element is proposed.

Case B: A computer-based guided composition program has been devised by a university team and tested for secondary school age students in the university laboratory school. Several enthusiastic school administrators are now proposing to install the program regionally. A budget is proposed for equipment purchases and for teacher inservice training at the university. Program factor analysis indicated "guided composition" to be an unfamiliar educational technique for most teachers (Factor 1). Current administrative disagreements regarding computer choice, software design, and equipment security and maintenance also yields a "high-difficulty" rating for Factor 13. The university team has high prestige (Factor 22) but little leverage (Factor 23). After deliberation, a decision is made (a) to introduce guided composition techniques through a newsletter with sample reproducible paper and pencil exercises; (b) to form a town/gown consortium to test and promote the new guided composition program; and (c) to hold inservice training sessions in familiar and easy-to-reach local schools rather than at the university.

Case C: Following successful trial and piloting of a process-based academic writing curriculum in a university English Language Institute, a decision has been made to use such an approach on a wider scale. Program factor analysis indicates that there is a wide disparity among teachers as to what constitutes a "process-based approach" (Factor 1), that learners might resist such an approach because it differs strongly from their previous experience of how writing is taught and because it involves extensive use of peer feedback (Factor 8), that a less textbook-oriented curriculum would require more teacher as well as learner initiative (Factor 13), and that teacher turnover is high, with most new teachers having had little experience in teaching writing at this level (Factor 21). Deliberation resulted in the suggestion that the existing program be modified to involve more process-directed activities, that ongoing inservice training be provided, and that an orientation program be provided for students entering the program.

The use of an activity like this has several benefits. It helps planners at all levels to

1. conceptualize educational planning in a new way
2. find out what they don't know and need to know
3. focus on issues of feasibility in education renewal
4. become more sensitive to the concerns of other individuals and agencies involved in educational change

5. identify factors requiring more detailed analysis
6. plan allocation of time, energy, and resources.

Perhaps most critically, the exercise of group deliberation built around the profile helps individuals involved in planning and implementation to develop cohesiveness and a deliberative style that facilitates more difficult problem resolution in the teaching and learning tasks that lie ahead. This contrasts with the approach to educational design typically seen in the field of language teaching. Program or curriculum development in language teaching has not generally been viewed as an integrated and interdependent set of processes that involves careful data gathering, planning, experimentation, monitoring, consultation, and evaluation. Rather, simplistic solutions are often advocated that address only one dimension of the process, for example by advocating changes in teaching techniques, methods, learning styles, technologies, materials, or teacher preparation. If the field of second and foreign language teaching is to attain the degree of rigor found in other areas of education, however, a more comprehensive basis for educational practices is needed.

Discussion topics and activities

1. Examine the list of questions related to situation analysis on page 2. Suggest three different procedures for finding answers to the questions, in relation to a language program or language teaching situation you are familiar with. What are the advantages and disadvantages of each procedure?
2. Prepare a plan to carry out a communicative needs analysis for the following situations:
   a) A group of foreign doctors requires an intensive language course before doing observations at local hospitals.
   b) A group of recently arrived immigrants requires a course to prepare them for hotel work.
3. Prepare three examples of goals for each of the situations you discussed in question 2, and three objectives for each program. Then discuss any difficulties you had in developing statements of objectives.
4. Prepare a description of microskills relating to conversational ability at a basic social or survival level.
5. Compare the syllabuses in Appendixes 3–5. How do they differ?
6. Prepare a syllabus outline for the following topic, which is to be included in a conversation course: "Inviting someone to do something." Your syllabus outline (one or two pages in length) should cover one unit of instruction.

7. Examine an ESL or foreign language course book. What assumptions underly the book with respect to
   a) the syllabus?
   b) the role of the teacher?
   c) the roles of the learners?
   d) learning theory?
8. In groups, examine a language teaching situation or program you are familiar with, in terms of the factors contained in the Program Planning Profile (Figure 1). Then compare your assessments with other groups.

Appendix 1: Situation analysis

The following is part of a questionnaire that tries to identify the learner's needs and preferred modes of learning.

QUESTIONNAIRE 2: HOW DO YOU LIKE LEARNING?

Put a circle around your answer.

a) In class do you like learning
    1. individually   YES / NO
    2. in pairs?   YES / NO
    3. in small groups?   YES / NO
    4. in one large group?   YES / NO

b) Do you want to do homework?   YES / NO
    If so, how much time have you got for homework outside class hours?
    _____ hours a day
    or
    _____ hours a week
    How would you like to spend this time?
    1. Preparing for the next class?   YES / NO
    2. Reviewing the day's work?   YES / NO
    3. Doing some kind of activity based on your personal experience, work experience, or interests?   YES / NO

c) Do you want to
    1. spend all your learning time in the classroom?   YES / NO
    or...
    2. spend some time in the classroom and some time practising your English with people outside?   YES / NO
    3. spend some time in the classroom and some time getting to know your city and the Australian way of life, e.g., by visiting Parliament, government offices, migrant resource centres, places of interest, work, entertainment, and so on?   YES / NO

d) Do you like learning
    1. by memory?   YES / NO
    2. by problem solving?   YES / NO
    3. by getting information for yourself?   YES / NO
    4. by listening?   YES / NO
    5. by reading?   YES / NO
    6. by copying off the board?   YES / NO
    7. by listening and taking notes?   YES/ NO

	8. by reading and making notes?	YES / NO
	9. by repeating what you hear?	YES / NO
	Put a cross next to the three things that you find most useful.	

e) When you speak do you want to be corrected
   1. immediately, in front of everyone? YES / NO
   or...
   2. later, at the end of the activity, in front of everyone? YES / NO
   or...
   3. later, in private? YES / NO

f) Do you mind if other students sometimes correct your written work? YES / NO
   Do you mind if the teacher sometimes asks you to correct your own work? YES / NO

g) Do you like learning from
   1. television/video/films? YES / NO
   2. radio? YES / NO

Appendix 2: Communicative needs analysis

The questionnaire from which this excerpt comes was formulated to "obtain a valid description of the kinds of writing tasks that are required of students ... during 'typical' coursework" at the university level (Bridgman and Carlson 1983; App. A).

For each of the following writing tasks, indicate how frequently each task might be assigned to students *per semester*. (Circle one number for each task.)

Writing tasks	Not at all	1–2 times per semester	3–6 times per semester	7 or more times per semester
1. Lab reports or descriptions of experiments conducted by the student or in class	0	1	2	3
2. Brief summaries of articles read (1–2 pages)	0	1	2	3
3. Brief research papers (5 pages or less)	0	1	2	3
4. Longer research papers (6 pages or more)	0	1	2	3
5. Creative writing (fiction, poetry, or drama)	0	1	2	3
6. Expository or critical writing unrelated to lab or library research	0	1	2	3
7. Exams with essay questions	0	1	2	3
8. Group writing projects	0	1	2	3
9. Case studies	0	1	2	3
10. Other (specify) _____	0	1	2	3
11. Other (specify) _____	0	1	2	3

Survey of Academic Writing Tasks Required of Graduate and Undergraduate Foreign Students by Brent Bridgeman and Sybil Carlson. Reprinted by permission of Educational Testing Service.

Appendix 3: Syllabus specifying activities

AREA FIVE

Required product: Oral/Written
Gathering of information, comments and ideas

Stimulus	*Situation*	*Notes*
1. Mode: Oral	(a) The host at a party suggests the game "Twenty Questions" and instructs guests on how it is played. As part of the game, ask your host pertinent questions so as to arrive at the answer he has in mind.	
	(b) As a father, you are worried about financial security for your famiy. You contact an insurance agent. In your conversation with him, find out which insurance scheme would best suit you.	
	(c) The manager of your insurance firm informs you that a client's car has been damaged in an accident and that he wants you to look into the matter immediately. Contact your client and ask him about the details and circumstances of the accident.	
	(d) A famous boxer has just arrived in this country. At the press conference at the airport, question him on his background and experiences.	
	(e) You want to buy a new car, and apart from setting your mind on a certain make, you have no idea of the attributes of the various models. Contact the sales representative of the nearest outlet and ask him about the various models available and details of them.	
	(f) You are in Hong Kong and would like to stay there for an extended period. Contact the manager of a suitable hotel and enquire about discounts for a long stay.	
	(g) You work in the survey department and have been assigned the task of finding out the spending habits of various households. Interview the heads of households and ask questions on their monthly expenditure.	

(h) As an employee in an oil firm, you would like to find out how people react to increases in the price of petrol. Interview several consumers and ask them in what ways the cost of petrol affects their travelling habits.

This excerpt is reprinted with permission from *English Language Syllabus in Malaysian Schools*, p. 46, © Hakcipta Kementerian Pelajaran Malaysia, 1975.

Appendix 4: Syllabus specifying content

Topic:: HOUSE and HOME

Level: POST-ELEMENTARY

SITUATION	FUNCTION	ACTUAL LANGUAGE	LANGUAGE PATTERNS and TENSES
Getting things connected e.g. gas, phone, TV Rent – payment, contract Buying furniture – second-hand, markets, auctions, small ads Paying bills – when and how At the door: milkman, postman, dustman, meter men, salesmen Repairs – plumber, electrician Making appointments Electoral Register	Understanding and asking for information Understanding directions and local information Expressing intentions Declining Giving information Making requests to	I'm looking for a large wardrobe. What sort of price did you have in mind? Have you got anything cheaper? I am moving to . . . . Can I have the gas/electricity connec-ted, please? What's your address? It's £70 deposit. Hello, I'm the . . . . I've come to read the meter. Could I see your identification, please? Where can I get a . . .? Are you interested in . . .? No, not today, thank you.	I'm looking for . . . . Have you got . . .? Could I have . . .? Can I . . .? Can you tell me . . .? Would you like . . .? Sorry, I . . . . Comparatives/adjectives Where can I . . .? (+ infinitive without to)

LEXIS	LITERACY	SYSTEM	AIDS and MATERIALS
Names of household items, including plugs, etc. Equipment Names of local institutions e.g. clinic, library	Reading bills, final demands, meters and filling in esti-mated bills, checking meter readings Library – Section headings Form-filling Reading contracts	Types of shops best for certain items Where to buy what Use of telephone for buying, inquiring Filing bills and receipts Guarantees What is delivered – milk, etc. How and when to pay bills Where to get local information – library, rent officer, Citizen's Advice Bureau, Legal Centre Asking for identification from strangers at the door Meaning of deposit Meaning of electoral register	Simplified maps of locality – grading up to actual maps Simplified and graded gas bills and meter readings '7 Days a Week' Pack Tapes – of dialogues in the situations

Reproduced from *Lessons from the Vietnamese* with permission from the National Extension College Trust Ltd.

Appendix 5: Syllabus specifying topics and competencies

TOPIC: TIME AND DATES – INSTRUCTIONAL UNIT 4   Level 1 – Survival ESL

COMPETENCIES: 8. Name, read and write months and their abbreviations. 9. Read and write dates in both words and numbers. 10. Ask about and give dates when asked. 11. Use a calendar.

SITUATION: Talking to co-worker or answering questions at Public Aid office, etc.

Listening ↔ Speaking	Reading	Writing	Grammatical structure focus	Vocabulary	Culture notes	Possible materials
What's the date (today)? (It's) X. (mo./day/yr.)	Months and their abbreviations	date and birthdate in word and number form (*August 10, 1984* = 8/10/84)	Wh-questions (what, when?)	Months and their abbreviations	Month precedes day in U.S. usage.	ANS pp. 13–14, 69
What's your birthdate? (It's) X (mo./day/yr.)	day date		Numbers, cardinal and ordinal	day date month (mo.)	On forms "date" means today's date.	ANS1 pp. 41, 47–53
When's your birthday? (It's) X. (mo./day)	month (mo.) year (yr.) birthdate			year (yr.) birthdate birthday	For bureaucratic purposes, knowledge of one's own birthdate and one's family's birthdates is essential.	ANS2 pp. 30–32, 58
What date is/was this/next/last *Friday?* The 3rd. (ordinal number)				calendar		EAC p. 19
Other questions requiring a date as answer (*When*				this next last		

Appendix 5 (continued)

TOPIC: TIME AND DATES – INSTRUCTIONAL UNIT 4   Level 1 – Survival ESL

COMPETENCIES: 8. Name, read and write months and their abbreviations. 9. Read and write dates in both words and numbers. 10. Ask about and give dates when asked. 11. Use a calendar.

SITUATION: Talking to co-worker or answering questions at Public Aid office, etc.

Listening ↔ Speaking	Reading	Writing	Grammatical structure focus	Vocabulary	Culture notes	Possible materials
did you come to the U.S.?, etc.).					Socially, birthdays are important in the U.S., and are usually celebrated with family and friends.	

Reprinted with permission from L. Mrowicki, R. Jones, and C. Porter, no date, *Project Work English*, *Competency-Based Curriculum*, Northwest Educational Cooperative, Des Plaines, Ill. Chicago: Department of Public Aid.

2 Beyond methods

In Chapter 1, methodology in teaching was described as the activities, tasks, and learning experiences used by the teacher within the teaching and learning process. Methodology was seen to have a theoretical basis in the teacher's assumptions about (a) language and second language learning, (b) teacher and learner roles, and (c) learning activities and instructional materials. These assumptions and beliefs provide the basis for the conscious or unconscious decision making that underlies the moment-to-moment processes of teaching. Methodology is not therefore something fixed, a set of rigid principles and procedures that the teacher must conform to. Rather it is a dynamic, creative, and exploratory process that begins anew each time the teacher encounters a group of learners. Teaching as an exploratory process is different from the approach to teaching seen in many teacher preparation programs or language teaching programs, where particular instructional methods, such as the Silent Way, Total Physical Response, or the Natural Approach, are presented as models to be imitated and internalized. In this chapter, these two approaches to teaching will be explored in more depth. The use of methods as the basis for instructional processes in a second language program will be compared with one that moves beyond methods and focuses on exploring the nature of effective classroom teaching and learning.

Approaching teaching in terms of methods

For many centuries the goal of language teachers has been to find the right method (Kelly 1969). The history of language teaching in the last hundred years has done much to support the impression that improvements in language teaching will result from improvements in the quality of methods, and that ultimately an effective language teaching method will be developed. Some breakthrough in linguistic theory or in second language acquisition research, it is assumed, will eventually unlock the secrets of second and foreign language learning. These will then be incorporated into a new supermethod that will solve the language teaching problem once and for all. Some believe that the supermethod has already been found, and that adoption of a method such as the Silent Way, Suggestopedia, or the Natural Approach will bring about dramatic improvements in language learning.

Common to all methods is a set of specifications for how teaching should be accomplished, derived from a particular theory of the nature of language and second language learning. Differences in the instructional specifications reflect differences in the theories underlying the methods. Some methods advocate an early emphasis on speaking as a basis for establishing basic language patterns. Others recommend that speaking be delayed until the learner has built up a receptive competence in the language. Some make use of memorized dialogues and texts; others require that learners attempt to communicate with each other as soon as possible using their own language resources. Common to all methods is a set of prescriptions on what teachers and learners should do in the language classroom. Prescriptions for the teacher include what material should be presented and when it should be taught and how, and prescriptions for learners include what approach they should take toward learning. Specific roles for teachers, learners, and instructional materials are hence established (Richards and Rodgers 1986). The teacher's job is to match his or her teaching style as well as the learners' learning styles to the method. Special training packages and programs are available for some methods to ensure that teachers do what they are supposed to do and teach according to the method.

Despite the appeal of methods, their past history is somewhat of an embarrassment. Studies of the effectiveness of specific methods have had a hard time demonstrating that the method itself, rather than other factors, such as the teacher's enthusiasm or the novelty of the new method, was the crucial variable. Likewise, observers of teachers using specific methods have reported that teachers seldom conform to the methods they are supposed to be following. Swaffar, Arens, and Morgan (1982), for example, investigated differences between what they termed rationalist and empiricist approaches to foreign language instruction. By a rationalist approach they refer to process-oriented approaches in which language is seen as an interrelated whole, where language learning is a function of comprehension preceding production, and where it involves critical thinking and the desire to communicate. Empiricist approaches focus on the four discrete language skills. Would classroom practices reflect such differences? "One consistent problem is whether or not teachers involved in presenting materials created for a particular method are actually reflecting the underlying philosophies of these methods in their classroom practices" (Swaffar et al. 1982: 25). Swaffar et al. found that many of the distinctions used to contrast methods, particularly those based on classroom activities, did not exist in actual practice:

Methodological labels assigned to teaching activities are, in themselves, not informative, because they refer to a pool of classroom practices which are used uniformly. The differences among major methodologies are to be found in the ordered hierarchy, the priorities assigned to tasks. (1982: 31)

Methods hence make assumptions about the nature of teaching that are not based on study of the process of teaching. The findings of Swaffar et al. account for the difficulty teacher supervisors often have in recognizing which method a teacher is following. Nevertheless, the future for methods continues to look good. Several new ones have appeared in recent years, and at conferences where salespersons for the new methods are present, teachers flock to hear presentations on the current super-methods. Yet there are serious limitations in conceptualizing teaching in terms of methods.

The basic problem is that methods present a predetermined, packaged deal for teachers that incorporates a static view of teaching. In this view specific teacher roles, learner roles, and teaching/learning activities and processes are imposed on teachers and learners. Studies of classroom events, however, have demonstrated that teaching is not static or fixed in time but is a dynamic, interactional process in which the teacher's "method" results from the processes of interaction between the teacher, the learners, and the instructional tasks and activities over time (Chall 1967; Dunkin and Biddle 1974; Swaffar et al. 1982). Attempts to find general methods that are suitable for all teachers and all teaching situations reflect an essentially negative view of teachers, one which implies that since the quality of teachers cannot be guaranteed, the contribution of the individual teacher should be minimized by designing teacher-proof methods. The assumption that underlies general, all-purpose methods is hence essentially this: Teachers cannot be trusted to teach well. Left to their own devices, teachers will invariably make a mess of things. A method, because it imposes a uniform set of teaching roles, teaching styles, teaching strategies, and teaching techniques on the teacher, will not be affected by the variations that are found in individual teaching skill and teaching style in the real world.

Researchers who have investigated the nature of teaching, however, have proposed a different view of teaching (Good 1979; Elliot 1980; Tikunoff 1985). They begin with the assumption that teachers (rather than methods) do make a difference; that teachers work in ways that are, to an extent, independent of methods; and that the characteristics of effective teaching can be determined. Other researchers have turned their attention to learners and sought to determine what characterizes effective learning. This requires a different approach to teaching, one in which teachers are involved in observing and reflecting upon their own teaching as well as the learning behaviors of their students.

The nature of effective teaching

Teacher strategies

Every teacher aims to be an effective teacher. The concept of effective teaching is a somewhat elusive one, however. Can it be determined from the teacher's behavior, the learner's behavior, classroom interaction, or the results of learning? Researchers have attempted to operationalize the notion of effective teaching by describing it as teaching that produces higher-than-predicted gains on standardized achievement tests (Good 1979). Studies of teacher effectiveness have dealt mainly with first language classrooms and with the teaching of reading and math. One major study has dealt with effective teachers in bilingual programs (Tikunoff et al. 1980; see also Chapter 8). These studies are characterized by detailed observation of teachers performing instructional activities in the classroom in an attempt to isolate the qualities and skills of effective teachers.

In a comprehensive survey of the research on effective schooling, Blum (1984: 3–6) summarizes effective classroom practices as follows:

1. Instruction is guided by a preplanned curriculum.
2. There are high expectations for student learning.
3. Students are carefully oriented to lessons.
4. Instruction is clear and focused.
5. Learning progress is monitored closely.
6. When students don't understand, they are retaught.
7. Class time is used for learning.
8. There are smooth and efficient classroom routines.
9. Instructional groups formed in the classroom fit instructional needs.
10. Standards for classroom behavior are high.
11. Personal interactions between teachers and students are positive.
12. Incentives and rewards for students are used to promote excellence.

Several dimensions of teaching have been found to account for differences between effective and ineffective instruction (Doyle 1977; Good 1979). These include classroom management, structuring, tasks, and grouping.

CLASSROOM MANAGEMENT

Classroom management refers to the ways in which student behavior, movement, and interaction during a lesson are organized and controlled by the teacher to enable teaching to take place most effectively. Good managerial skills on the part of the teacher are an essential component of good teaching. In a well-managed class, discipline problems are few, and learners are actively engaged in learning tasks and activities; this contributes to high motivation and expectations for success. Evertson, Anderson, and Brophy (1978) found that it was possible to identify teachers with managerial problems in the first few days of the school year, that such problems continued throughout the year, and that managerial skills in the classroom were related to levels of student involvement.

STRUCTURING

A lesson reflects the concept of *structuring* when the teacher's intentions are clear and instructional activities are sequenced according to a logic that students can perceive. Classroom observations and studies of lesson protocols indicate that sometimes neither the teacher nor the learners understood what the intentions of an activity were, why an activity occurred when it did, what directions they were supposed to follow, or what the relationship between one activity and another was. Hence, it may not have been clear what students needed to focus on to complete a task successfully. Fisher et al. (1980) conclude that students "pay attention more when the teacher spends time discussing the goals or structures of the lesson and/or giving directions about what the students are to do" (p. 26). Berliner (1984) likewise suggests that "structuring affects attention rate: it is sometimes not done at all, sometimes it is done only minimally, and sometimes it is overdone" (p. 63).

TASKS

Tasks, or activity structures, refer to activities that teachers assign to attain particular learning objectives. For any given subject at any given level, a teacher uses a limited repertoire of tasks that essentially define that teacher's methodology of teaching. These might include completing worksheets, reading aloud, dictation, quickwriting, and practicing dialogues. According to Tikunoff (1985), class tasks vary according to three types of demands they make on learners: *response mode demands* (the kind of skills they demand, such as knowledge, comprehension, application, analysis/synthesis, evaluation); *interactional mode demands* (the rules governing how classroom tasks are accomplished, such as individually, in a group, or with the help of the teacher); and *task complexity demands* (how difficult the learner perceives the task to be).

Teachers have to make decisions not only about the appropriate kinds of tasks to assign to learners, but also about the *order of tasks* (the sequence in which tasks should be introduced); *pacing* (how much time learners should spend on tasks); *products* (whether the product or result of a task is expected to be the same for all students); *learning strategies* (what learning strategies will be recommended for particular tasks); and *materials* (what sources and materials to use in completing a task) (Tikunoff 1985).

The concept of tasks has been central to studies of effective teaching. The amount of time students spend actively engaged on learning tasks is directly related to learning (Good and Beckerman 1978). For example, Teacher A and Teacher B are both teaching the same reading lesson. In Teacher A's class, learners are actively engaged in reading tasks for 75% of the lesson, the remaining time being occupied with noninstructional activities such as taking breaks, lining up, distributing books, homework, and making arrangements for future events. Students in Teacher B's class, however, are actively involved in reading for only 55% of the lesson. Not surprisingly, studies of time-on-task have found that the more time students spend studying content, the better they learn it. In one study (Stallings and Kaskowitz 1974), the students with the highest levels of achievement in a reading program were spending about 50% more time actively engaged in reading activities than the children with the lowest achievement gains. Good teaching is hence said to be task oriented. Effective teachers also monitor performance on tasks, providing feedback on how well tasks have been completed.

GROUPING

A related dimension of effective teaching is the *grouping* of learners to carry out instructional tasks, and the relation between grouping arrangement and achievement. An effective teacher understands how different kinds of grouping (such as seat work, pair work, discussion, reading circle, or lecture) can impede or promote learning. Webb (1980) found that the middle-ability child suffers a loss of achievement, while the low-ability child shows some gains in achievement in mixed-ability groups, compared with what would be expected if both were in uniform-ability groups. Tikunoff (1985) cites Good and Marshall's findings on groupings.

Good and Marshall (1984) found that students in low-ability reading groups in the early grades received very little challenge, thus perceiving of themselves as unable to read. In addition, a long-range result of interacting most frequently with only other students of low-ability in such groups was an inability to respond to the demands of more complex instructional activities. Ironically, Good pointed out that the very strategy used to presumably help low-ability youngsters with their reading problems – pull-out programs in which teachers worked with small groups of these students outside the regular classroom – exacerbated the problem. Demands in the special reading groups were very different from those in the regular classroom and at a much lower level of complexity, so low-ability students were not learning to respond to high level demands that would help them participate competently in their regular classrooms. (p. 56)

The research findings suggest therefore that effective teaching depends on such factors as time-on-task, feedback, grouping and task decisions, classroom management, and structuring. Although the concept of effective teaching evolved from studies of content teaching, Tikunoff's (1983) major study of effective teaching in bilingual education programs has examined the extent to which it also applies to other contexts, such as bilingual and ESL classrooms.

EFFECTIVE TEACHING IN BILINGUAL CLASSROOMS

Tikunoff (1983) suggests that three kinds of competence are needed for the student of limited English proficiency (LEP): *participative competence,* the ability "to respond appropriately to class demands and the procedural rules for accomplishing them" (p. 4); *interactional competence,* the ability "to respond both to classroom rules of discourse and social rules of discourse, interacting appropriately with peers and adults while accomplishing class tasks" (p. 4); and *academic competence,* the ability "to acquire new skills, assimilate new information, and construct new concepts" (p. 4). Furthermore, to be functionally proficient in the classroom, the student must be able to utilize these competences to perform three major functions: (a) to decode and understand both task expectations and new information; (b) to engage appropriately in completing tasks, with high accuracy; and (c) to obtain accurate feedback with relation to completing tasks accurately (p. 5).

In his Significant Bilingual Instructional Features (SBIF) descriptive study, Tikunoff (1983) collected data to find out how effective teachers in bilingual education programs organize instruction, structure teaching activities, and enhance student performance on tasks. Teachers were interviewed to determine their instructional philosophies, goals, and the demands they would structure into class tasks. Teachers were clearly able to specify class task demands and intended outcomes and to indicate what LEP students had to do to be functionally proficient. Case studies of teachers were undertaken in which teachers were observed during instruction, with three observers collecting data for the teacher and for four target LEP students. Teachers were interviewed again after instruction.

An analysis of data across the case studies revealed a clear linkage between (1) teachers' ability to clearly specify the intent of instruction, and a belief that students could achieve accuracy in instructional tasks, (2) the organization and delivery of instruction such that tasks and institutional demands reflected this intent, requiring intended student responses, and (3) the fidelity of

41

student consequences with intended outcomes. In other words, teachers were able to describe clearly what instruction would entail, to operationalize these specifications, and to produce the desired results in terms of student performance. (p. 9)

This approach to teaching is one in which methodological principles are developed from studying the classroom practices and processes actually employed by effective teachers. Good teaching is not viewed as something that results from using Method X or Method Y, or something that results from the teacher modifying teaching behaviors to match some external set of rules and principles. Rather, it results from the teacher's active control and management of the processes of teaching, learning, and communication within the classroom and from an understanding of these processes. The classroom is seen as a place where there is ongoing and dynamic interaction between the teacher's instructional goals, learners' purposes, classroom tasks and activities, the teacher's instructional activities and behaviors, student behaviors in completing assigned tasks, and learning outcomes.

In the bilingual classrooms observed in Tikunoff's study, effective teaching was found to reflect the degree to which the teacher is able to successfully communicate his or her intentions, maintain students' engagement in instructional tasks, and monitor students' performance on tasks. In classrooms where different instructional goals are present and different aspects of second language proficiency are being addressed, the characteristics of effective teaching in those settings cannot be inferred merely from reading about the theoretical principles underlying the method or approach the teacher is supposed to be following. Rather, classroom observation of teachers who are achieving higher-than-predicted levels of achievement in their learners, or who are assessed as performing at high levels of effectiveness according to other criteria, provides the data from which profiles of effective teachers in listening, reading, writing, speaking, and other kinds of classes can be developed. An example of this approach is given in Chapter 5, where a case study is presented of an effective teacher in a second language reading class.

Learner strategies

The approach to teaching in which methodology is developed from study of classroom practices attributes a primary role to the teacher in the teaching/learning process. Successful learning is viewed as dependent upon the teacher's control and management of what takes place in the classroom. However, what the teacher does is only half of the picture. The other half concerns what learners do to achieve successful learning, or *learner strategies*. Prompted by the awareness that learners may succeed despite the teacher's methods and techniques rather than because of them, researchers as well as teachers have begun to look more closely at learners themselves in an attempt to discover how successful learners achieve their results (O'Malley et al. 1985a, b; Willing 1985).

Studies of learner strategies attempt to identify the specific techniques and strategies learners use to facilitate their own learning (Oxford 1985b). The focus is on the particular cognitive operations, processes, procedures, and heuristics that learners apply to the task of learning a second language. Given any language learning task, such as understanding a lecture, reading a text, writing a composition, understanding the meaning of a new grammatical or lexical item, or preparing a written summary of a text, a number of strategies are available to a learner to help carry out the task. But what is the practical value of knowing which particular strategies a learner employed?

Just as research on effective teaching has identified the kinds of teaching behaviors that appear to account for superior teaching, so research on effective learning seeks to identify the kinds of learning behaviors that can best facilitate learning. Good language learners seem to be successful because they have a better understanding of and control over their own learning than less successful learners. Use of inappropriate learning strategies has been found to account for the poor performance of learners on many classroom learning tasks (Hosenfeld 1979). It should therefore be possible to improve student performance on learning tasks by identifying successful approaches to learning and by directing learners toward these kinds of strategies. Research on learner strategies in second language learning hence seeks to identify the strategies employed by successful learners and then to teach those strategies to other learners in order to improve their language learning capacities (Hosenfeld 1977; Cohen and Aphek 1980; Chamot and O'Malley 1984). The premises underlying Cohen and Aphek's work, for example, are:

Some language learners are more successful than others.
Some aspects of the learning process are conscious and others are not.
Less successful learners can use successful strategies consciously to accelerate learning.
Teachers can promote the use of learning strategies.
Learners can become the best judges of how they learn most effectively, both in and out of classes.

The field of learner strategy research in second language learning is hence now an important domain of classroom research, and differs substantially from previous research in this area. Earlier work on learning strategies lacked a sound theoretical basis and consisted largely of lists of features that good language learners were assumed to possess. These lists were developed from interviews with successful language learners (e.g., Rubin 1975, 1981; Stern 1975; Naiman et al. 1978). Willing (1987:

275) points out that "while such generalizations have their usefulness as a help in understanding the process of language learning from the point of view of the learner, they do not immediately yield prescriptions for teaching."

More recent work on learner strategies has attempted to yield more usable results by making use of data obtained from a broader range of sources, such as classroom observation, "think-aloud" procedures (in which learners record their thoughts and observations as they perform different tasks), interviews, self-reports employing note-taking and diaries, questionnaires, as well as controlled experimental studies designed to investigate specific cognitive processes (e.g., Heuring 1984). These kinds of approaches are yielding information of greater practical value. For example, Cohen (cited in Oxford 1985a) lists six strategies used by successful language learners:

1. Attention-enhancing strategies, such as responding silently to tasks asked of other students in class
2. Use of a variety of background sources, including knowledge of the world, knowledge of the given topic, awareness of stress and tone of voice of the speaker, perception of the speaker's body language, and cues from earlier parts of the conversation in the effort to decode communicative meaning
3. Oral production tricks, such as avoiding unfamiliar topics, paraphrasing, and asking for help
4. Vocabulary learning techniques, such as making associations, attending to the meaning of parts of the word, noting the structure of the word, placing the word in a topical group with similar words, visualizing or contextualizing it, linking it to the situation in which it appears, creating a mental image of it, and associating some physical sensation to it
5. Reading or text-processing strategies, such as clarifying the communicative purpose of the text, distinguishing important points from trivia, skipping around to get an overall conceptual picture, using substantive and linguistic background knowledge, reading in broad phrases rather than word for word, relying on contextual clues, making ongoing summaries, and looking for emphasis and cohesion markers in the text
6. Writing techniques such as focusing on simply getting ideas down on paper instead of trying for perfection right away; purposefully using parallel structures and other means of enhancing cohesion; and writing multiple drafts.

Willing (1987: 278–9) notes that strategies are essentially "methods employed by the person for processing input language information in such a way as to gain control of it, thus enabling the assimilation of that information by the self." Strategies are hence viewed as ways of managing the complex information that the learner is receiving about the target language.

Wenden (1983) interviewed adult language learners about how they organized their language learning experiences and found that they asked themselves eight kinds of questions.

Question	*Decision*
1. How does this language work?	Learners make judgments about the linguistic and sociolinguistic codes.
2. What's it like to learn a language?	Learners make judgments about how to learn a language and about what language learning is like.
3. What should I learn and how?	Learners decide upon linguistic objectives, resources, and use of resources.
4. What should I emphasize?	Learners decide to give priority to special linguistic items.
5. How should I change?	Learners decide to change their approach to language learning.
6. How am I doing?	Learners determine how well they use the language and diagnose their needs.
7. What am I getting out of this?	Learners determine if an activity or strategy is useful.
8. How am I responsible for learning? How is language learning affecting me?	Learners make judgments about how to learn a language and about what language learning is like.

O'Malley et al. have investigated the use of strategies by ESL learners both in and out of classrooms (O'Malley et al. 1985a, b; O'Malley and Chamot 1989). ESL students and their teachers were interviewed about the strategies learners used on specific language learning tasks, and the learners were observed in ESL classrooms. They were also asked about their use of English in communicative situations outside the classroom. A total of twenty-six different kinds of learning strategies were identified.

In a follow-up study, high school ESL students were given training in the use of particular strategies in order to determine if it would improve their effectiveness as language learners and their performance on vocabulary, listening, and speaking tasks. Strategies were compared across proficiency levels and with learners of different language backgrounds. Students were given training in the use of specific strategies for particular language learning tasks. Results supported the notion that learners can be taught to use more effective learning strategies (O'Malley et al. 1985a, b):

Strategies training was successfully demonstrated in a natural teaching environment with second language listening and speaking tasks. This indicates that classroom instruction on learning strategies with integrative language skills can facilitate learning. (O'Malley et al. 1985a: 577)

Phillips (1975) investigated how learners approach reading tasks and identified strategies employed by good and poor readers. She employed a "think-aloud" procedure to investigate readers' strategies in dealing with unknown vocabulary. From her students' descriptions Phillips found that strategies used by efficient readers included categorizing words grammatically, interpreting grammatical operations, and recognizing cognates and root words. Hosenfeld (1977, 1984) used similar techniques in studying processes employed by foreign language readers when encountering unfamiliar words. In one study (Hosenfeld 1977), some of the differences between those with high and low scores on a reading proficiency test were these: High scorers tended to keep the meaning of the passage in mind, read in broad phrases, skip unessential words, and guess meanings of unknown words from context; low scorers tended to lose the meaning of sentences as soon as they decoded them, read word by word or in short phrases, rarely skip words, and turn to the glossary when they encountered new words. In addition successful readers tended to identify the grammatical categories of words, could detect word-order differences in the foreign language, recognized cognates, and used the glossary only as a last resort (Hosenfeld 1984: 233). Hosenfeld found that unsuccessful readers could be taught the lexical strategies of successful readers, confirming Wenden's observation that "ineffective learners are inactive learners. Their apparent inability to learn is, in fact, due to their not having an appropriate repertoire of learning strategies" (1985: 7).

Studies of how learners approach writing tasks have also focused on the effectiveness of the processes learners employ (Raimes 1985). Lapp (1984) summarizes some of the research findings on differences between skilled and unskilled writers with respect to rehearsing and prewriting behaviors (what a writer does before beginning writing), drafting and writing processes (how the writer actually composes a piece of writing), and revising behaviors (revisions and corrections the writer makes). (See Chapter 6, Appendix, for a list of differences between unskilled and skilled writers.)

Research findings on learner strategies in reading and writing classes (e.g., Heuring 1984) suggest that teachers need to evaluate their teaching strategies on an ongoing basis, to determine if they are promoting effective or ineffective learning strategies in learners. (Ways in which teachers can gather information of this kind are discussed in Chapter 7.) As is suggested in Chapter 6, many commonly employed techniques in the teaching of writing, such as outlining or writing from a rhetorical model, might well inhibit rather than encourage the development of effective writing skills, because they direct the learner's attention to the form and mechanics of writing too early in the writing process.

In order to present information about learning strategies to students, strategies need to be operationalized in the form of specific techniques (see Fraser and Skibicki 1987); however, there is no consensus yet concerning how to approach the teaching of learning strategies. As with other aspects of language teaching, the issue of whether strategies are best "learned" or "acquired" is a central one. Some researchers advocate a direct approach. This involves explicit training in the use of specific strategies and teaching students to consciously monitor their own strategies (e.g., O'Malley et al. 1985a, b; Russo and Stewner-Manzanares 1985). Others favor a more indirect approach in which strategies are incorporated into other kinds of learning content. Fraser and Skibicki (1987) describe the development of self-directed learning materials for adult migrant learners in Australia, which focus on specific strategies in different skill areas. A related issue concerns whether the focus of teacher intervention should be to provide additional strategies to learners or merely to help the learner develop a better awareness of and control over existing strategies. Willing (1987: 277) observes that despite the recent amount of attention to learning strategies, some serious issues still await resolution:

1. Current notions of learning strategies lack conceptual coherence...
2. Learning strategies as currently described have been identified more or less in isolation and on a purely empirical and arbitrary basis and have not been related to an overall view of learning...
3. There has been little systematic work on placing learning strategies within a broader description of the nature and meaning of learning itself...
4. There has been little effort to relate the notion of learning strategies (within a general learning theory) to current ideas about second language acquisition.

In addition, there has been little attempt to relate theories of learning strategies to more general theories of teaching, such as the one discussed previously.

Summary

Two approaches to language teaching have been discussed and contrasted. One conceptualizes teaching as application of a teaching method, in which both the teacher and the learner are approached on the terms of the method promoter, educational theorist, or applied linguist. The assumptions or theory underlying the method provide the starting point for an instructional design that is subsequently imposed on teachers and learners. An attempt is then made to make the teacher's and learner's classroom behaviors match the specifications of the method. This can be contrasted with an approach that starts with the observable processes of classroom teaching and learning, from which methodological principles and practices in language teaching are derived. Observation can yield two categories of information:

1. The study of effective teaching provides information about how effective teachers organize and deliver instruction. This relates to classroom management skills, and to the strategies teachers use to present instructional goals, structure learning tasks and activities, monitor learning, and provide feedback on it.
2. The study of effective learning provides information about the learning strategies effective learners apply to the process of using and learning a second and foreign language.

However, a word of caution is in order, since the goal of this approach is not simply to arrive at a set of general principles that can be taught to teachers and learners. This of course would be to come full circle, and would simply replace one "method" with another. The approach advocated here starts with the assumption that the investigation of effective teaching and learning strategies is a central and ongoing component of the process of teaching. This is the core of a process-oriented methodology of teaching.

This approach implies a redefinition of the role of the teacher. Teachers are not viewed merely as "performers," who carry out the role prescribed by the method or apply an externally derived set of principles to their teaching. Teachers are seen rather as investigators of both their own classroom practices and those of the learners. Much of the effort to determine what constitutes effective teaching and learning is initiated by the teacher. Through regular observation of their own classes and through analysis and reflection, teachers can obtain valuable feedback about the effectiveness of their own teaching. At the same time they can develop a better understanding of the principles that account for effective teaching and learning in their own classrooms. (Procedures for carrying out teacher self-monitoring are discussed in Chapter 7.) In the domain of learning strategies, the teacher also has an important role to play. The teacher is initially an observer and investigator of the learners' learning behaviors and subsequently provides feedback on the kind of strategies that are most successful for carrying out specific learning tasks. Relevant concerns for the teacher thus focus not on the search for the best method, but rather on the circumstances and conditions under which more effective teaching and learning are accomplished.

Discussion topics and activities

1. Compare two language teaching methods you are familiar with. How do they differ with respect to:
   a) assumptions about second language learning?
   b) teacher and learner roles?
   c) role of instructional materials?
   d) kinds of instructional activities employed?
   To what extent do the two methods prescribe roles and behaviors for teachers and learners?
2. Why do you think name-brand methods seem to be an attraction for many teachers? Do you think methods help or hinder teachers?
3. If possible, find a class where a teacher is using a particular method and observe the teacher in action. To what extent is the teacher "following" the method? In what ways does the teacher depart from the method? Can you suggest why?
4. Have you experienced an effective teacher in any of your classes? Prepare a list of reasons that you think account for the teacher's effectiveness. Then compare your list with the list quoted from Blum, on page 38.
5. Observe a class and notice how the teacher deals with classroom management and grouping. Were there any aspects of the teacher's treatment of these issues that you would have handled differently?
6. Prepare a set of questions you could use to interview a teacher in order to explore the teacher's philosophy of teaching and how the teacher achieves his or her goals. Then use your questions to interview a teacher. Compare the information with information obtained by other students. How similar or different is the information you obtained?
7. In groups, compare your experiences in studying foreign languages and consider the questions cited from Wenden on page 45. Did you ask yourself similar questions? Can you provide examples of how questions like these affected your approach to learning?
8. Do you think it is possible to teach strategies to learners? Select a strategy, operationalize it, and suggest how it could be taught.

3 Designing instructional materials for teaching listening comprehension

In Chapter 1 the role of instructional materials in the language curriculum was discussed, and it was argued that effective instructional materials in language teaching are based on theoretically sound learning principles, are appropriate to the learners' needs, provide examples of how language is used, and provide opportunities for communicative and authentic language use. In this chapter, some of the theoretical principles underlying the design of listening materials will be examined. Any approach to the design of listening comprehension materials and classroom activities reflects a view of the nature of listening and the processes it involves. An understanding of the role of bottom-up and top-down processes in listening is central to any theory of listening comprehension, as well as recognition of the differences between the interactional and transactional dimensions of language use and how these affect listening. In this chapter, these views of listening are first elaborated and then applied to the design of instructional materials and activities for the teaching of listening comprehension.

Listening processes: bottom-up and top-down processing

Two distinct kinds of processes are involved in listening comprehension, which are sometimes referred to as "bottom-up" and "top-down" processing (Chaudron and Richards 1986). Bottom-up processing refers to the use of incoming data as a source of information about the meaning of a message. From this perspective, the process of comprehension begins with the message received, which is analyzed at successive levels of organization – sounds, words, clauses, and sentences – until the intended meaning is arrived at. Comprehension is thus viewed as a process of decoding. Examples of bottom-up processes in listening include the following:

1. scanning the input to identify familiar lexical items
2. segmenting the stream of speech into constituents – for example, in order to recognize that "abookofmine" consists of four words

3. using phonological cues to identify the information focus in an utterance
4. using grammatical cues to organize the input into constituents – for example, in order to recognize that in "the book which I lent you" [the book] and [which I lent you] are the major constituents rather than [the book which I] and [lent you].

The listener's lexical and grammatical competence in a language provides the basis for bottom-up processing. A person's lexical competence serves as a mental dictionary to which incoming words are referred for meaning assignment. Grammatical competence can be thought of as a set of strategies that are applied to the analysis of incoming data. Clark and Clark (1977: 49) summarize this view of listening comprehension in the following way:

1. They [listeners] take in raw speech and retain a phonological representation of it in "working memory."
2. They immediately attempt to organize the phonological representation into constituents, identifying their content and function.
3. As they identify each constituent, they use it to construct underlying propositions, building continually onto a hierarchical representation of propositions.
4. Once they have identified the propositions for a constituent, they retain them in working memory and at some point purge memory of the phonological representation. In doing this, they forget the exact wording and retain the meaning.

Top-down processing, on the other hand, refers to the use of background knowledge in understanding the meaning of a message. Background knowledge may take several forms. It may be previous knowledge about the topic of discourse, it may be situational or contextual knowledge, or it may be knowledge stored in long-term memory in the form of "schemata" and "scripts" – plans about the overall structure of events and the relationships between them.

For example, if an adult was seated on a park bench reading aloud from a book to a group of enthralled young children, an observer would probably assume that the adult was reading a story – rather than, say, a recipe or a set of instructions on how to assemble a computer. This set of expectations for a particular kind of discourse is generated from the situation, from knowledge of a world populated by adults and children and typical interactions between them. On moving closer, the observer is able to confirm that the children are indeed listening to a story. Now the observer activates his or her "schema" for stories. This can be thought of as a set of expectations as to how the content of the discourse will develop:

Where does the story take place?
Who are the characters?
Around what event or events does the story turn?
What will the outcome be?

Much of people's knowledge of the world consists of knowledge about specific situations, the people one might expect to encounter in such situations, what those people's goals and purposes are, and how they typically accomplish them. In applying this prior knowledge about people and events to a particular situation, comprehension proceeds from the top down. The actual discourse that is heard is used to confirm expectations and to fill out the specific details. Examples of top-down processing in listening include:

assigning an interaction to part of a particular event, such as storytelling, joking, praying, complaining;
assigning places, persons, or things to categories;
inferring cause-and-effect relationships;
anticipating outcomes;
inferring the topic of a discourse;
inferring the sequence between events;
inferring missing details.

If the listener is unable to make use of top-down processing, an utterance or discourse may be incomprehensible. Bottom-up processing alone often provides an insufficient basis for comprehension. Consider the following narrative, for example. What is the topic?

Sally first tried setting loose a team of gophers. The plan backfired when a dog chased them away. She then entertained a group of teenagers and was delighted when they brought their motorcycles. Unfortunately, she failed to find a Peeping Tom listed in the Yellow Pages. Furthermore, her stereo system was not loud enough. The crab grass might have worked but she didn't have a fan that was sufficiently powerful. The obscene phone calls gave her hope until the number was changed. She thought about calling a door-to-door salesman but decided to hang up a clothesline instead. It was the installation of blinking neon lights across the street that did the trick. She eventually framed the ad from the classified section. (Stein and Albridge 1978)

At first the narrative is virtually incomprehensible. However, once a schema is provided to apply to the narrative – "Getting rid of a troublesome neighbor" – the reader can make use of top-down processing, and the elements of the story begin to fit into place.

When learners first encounter a foreign language, they depend heavily upon top-down processing. For example, imagine a foreigner who has taken up residence in Japan. The first time she joins a group of Japanese friends for a meal, she hears them utter something that sounds like

"Itadakemasu" before they begin eating. She has no idea if this is one word or three, or whether it refers to the food or to the participants. After repeated experiences of this kind, however, and observation of the position and function the utterance occupies within the speech event of "meal talk," she infers that it is some kind of pre-eating ritual, probably the equivalent of "Bon apetit." If she subsequently goes on to learn some Japanese, she will be able to apply her knowledge of Japanese words and grammar to the phrase to arrive at its literal meaning, which is "eat – going to." Initially, then, she is entirely dependent upon top-down processing – that is, the use of background knowledge – in working out the meaning of the utterance, and only later, when her linguistic competence has developed, can she analyze it from the bottom up.

This is how listening comprehension often takes place at the initial stages in second language learning. For example the Australian Adult Migrant Education Listening Proficiency Descriptions, which are derived from analysis of the listening difficulties of on-arrival migrants to Australia and which characterize listening skills across seven levels of proficiency, include the following information concerning listeners at the lowest levels of proficiency:

Level 0.5
No idea of syntactic relationships between words. Responds to isolated items and has to rely almost entirely on context to guess meaning.

Here the listener is unable to use bottom-up processing. Gradually, as language learning proceeds, the ability to use bottom-up processing emerges, as we see in the following descriptions of Levels 1, 2, and 3 in the Australian proficiency descriptions:

Level 1.
Little understanding of syntax. Meaning deduced from juxtaposition of words and context. Still responds to isolated words in connected speech... Speaker frequently forced to expand or paraphrase when listener's unfamiliarity with syntactic conventions causes misunderstanding.

Level 2
Beginning awareness of grammar but still relies heavily on stressed words and context to deduce meaning... Can follow very simple, slowly-spoken verbal instructions only if supported by context. Certain areas of English grammar tend to cause severe comprehension problems (e.g. tense marking, pronoun reference, subordination).

Level 3
Can understand some syntactic clues to meaning, but understanding of grammar very incomplete. In conversation, needs much more redundancy than

native speaker. Sometimes has to ask for clarification where syntax would make meaning clear to native speaker.

(Brindley, personal communication)

By the time the learner is at Level 4 or 5 on the proficiency scale, there is less dependence on context. Context is now used in association with the ability to process the message itself to work out unfamiliar meanings.

Fluent listening thus depends on the use of both top-down and bottom-up processing. The extent to which one or the other dominates reflects the degree of familiarity the listener has with the topic of discourse, the kind of background knowledge he or she can apply to the task, and the purposes for which he or she is listening. An experienced cook, for example, might listen to a radio chef describing a recipe for coq au vin merely to compare the chef's recipe with her own. She has a precise schema to apply to the task of listening and listens in order to register similarities or differences. She makes heavy use of top-down processes in listening to the radio program. A novice cook however, with little previous cooking experience and who is unfamiliar with coq au vin, will be required to listen with much greater attention, perhaps in order to write the recipe down. Here, far more bottom-up processing is required.

Listening purposes: interpersonal and transactional functions of language

As well as recognizing the fundamental difference between top-down and bottom-up processing in comprehending language, it is also necessary to recognize the very different purposes that listeners may have in different situations, and how these differences in purpose affect the way they go about listening. Numerous classifications exist of the different functions and purposes for which people use language; a simple but useful distinction made by Brown and Yule (1983) between interactional and transactional functions of language is used here.

Interactional functions of language

Interactional uses of language are those in which the primary purposes for communication are social. The emphasis is on creating harmonious interactions between participants rather than on communicating information. The goal for the participants is to make social interaction comfortable and nonthreatening and to communicate good will. Although information may be communicated in the process, the accurate and orderly presentation of information is not the primary purpose. Examples of interactional uses of language are greetings, making small talk, telling jokes, giving compliments, making casual "chat" of the kind used to pass time with friends or to make encounters with strangers comfortable. Brown and Yule suggest that language used in the interactional mode is *listener oriented*. Questions of "face" are central; hence interactional conversation is a kind of "work" that is done in order for speaker and hearer to maintain face and to respect the face put forward by others. This is what the sociologist Goffman (1976) referred to as "face work." For example, a foreman who sees a worker sweating profusely as he works on a difficult job remarks sympathetically, "It's hard work." Or a person waiting at a bus stop in a heavy downpour remarks to another person waiting, "Will it ever stop?" In both cases the speaker's primary purpose is not to inform the listener of the obvious but to be *identified* with the concerns of the other person (Wardhaugh 1985).

One of the rules of "face work" is that it should elicit agreement, hence the importance of small talk on "safe" topics, such as the weather, the beauty of gardens, the incompetence of politicians, and so on (Brown and Levinson 1978). Agreement creates harmony and diminishes the threat to the participants' face. Brown and Yule add that constant shifts of topic are also characteristic of this mode of talk, and illustrate this with an extract from a conversation between some people who have been talking about a couple who visit the area in the summer. (The + signs represent a short pause.)

A: you know but erm + they used to go out in erm August + they used to come + you know the lovely sunsets you get + at that time and
B: oh yes
C: there's a nice new postcard a nice – well I don't know how new it is + it's been a while since I've been here + of a sunset + a new one +
A: oh that's a lovely one isn't it
D: yes yes it was in one of the + calendars
A: yes that was last year's calendar it was on
D: was it last year's it was on + it was John Forgan who took that one
A: yes it's really lovely + this year's erm + the Anderson's house at Lenimore's in it + at em Thunderguy I should say +
D: they've sold their house
A: yes + the Andersons
B: oh have they
A: yes yes + erm + they weren't down last year at all +

(Brown and Yule 1983: 11–12)

This extract also demonstrates another aspect of interactional discourse – that since the conversation exists largely to satisfy the social needs of the participants at that time, it is extremely boring for an outsider to listen to.

The language teaching matrix

Most conversations are appallingly boring. It is the *participation* in such conversations which makes us such avid talkers, the "need to know" or the "need to tell" or the "need to be friendly." You can listen to hours and hours of recorded conversation without finding anything that interests you from the point of view of what the speakers are talking about or what they are saying about it. After all, their conversation was not intended for the overhearer. It was intended for them as participants. (Brown and Yule 1983: 82)

Likewise because such discourse is frequently between people who know each other and who share background knowledge about the topics introduced, a great deal is left unsaid. Conversations are embedded in context. Since the participants are able to fill out the details using top-down comprehension, it is not necessary to specify things very clearly. Interactional discourse is hence characterized by a high frequency of words for which a precise reference is not specified.

Transactional functions of language

Transactional uses of language are those in which language is being used primarily for communicating information. They are "message" oriented rather than "listener" oriented. Accurate and coherent communication of the message is important, as well as confirmation that the message has been understood. Explicitness and directness of meaning is essential, in comparison with the vagueness of interactional language. With transactional uses of language, coherence, content, and clarity are crucial. Brown and Yule observe that completion of some kind of real-world task often accompanies transactional uses of language, such as writing down a message or carrying out an instruction. Examples of language being used primarily for a transactional purpose include news broadcasts, lectures, descriptions, and instructions. Brown et al. (1984) suggest that this is the kind of talk that dominates classroom life:

Teacher: now + here we have a substance in which heat is moving along the rod from a hot end to a cold end + + can anybody tell me the name we give to such a substance – a substance in which heat can flow + + nobody can tell me that + well + it's called a conductor + + anybody ever heard of that word before? + good well + I'll put it on the blackboard for you + + it's called a conductor + what we are going to do today is have a look at some conductors. (Brown et al. 1984: 9)

Tikunoff (1985) suggests that effective pupil classroom participation requires command of language in both its interactional and transactional functions (see Chapter 8). Language in its interactional functions is needed in order to interact with the teacher and peers while accomplishing class tasks, and language in its transactional functions is needed in order to acquire new skills, assimilate new information, and construct new concepts. In many situations, both interactional and transactional functions are involved. At the doctor's, for example, the doctor may first use small talk to put the patient at ease, then switch to the transactional mode while asking for a description of the patient's medical problem.

The four-part classification of listening processes and listening purposes established previously can be used as a framework for comparing the different demands of different listening activities. Listening activities may be located at different positions within the following quadrant:

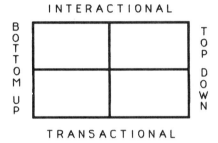

Consider a person listening to cocktail party banter, for example, during which friends greet each other, exchange compliments and other customary rituals, and engage in small talk on fleeting topics of no import to anyone present. Such an activity would be located in the following position on the quadrant:

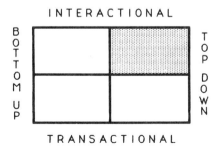

Now consider an experienced air traveler on an airplane listening to a flight attendant reading the air safety instructions before takeoff. This language would be located in the following position on the quadrant:

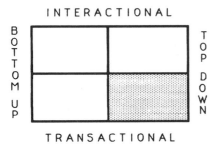

An activity that is transactional but that requires more use of bottom-up processing, such as a student driver receiving his or her first driving lesson from a driving instructor, would look like this on the quadrant:

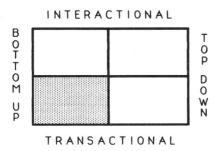

An example of bottom-up processing within an interactional situation would be a partygoer listening intently to someone telling a bad joke and trying to identify where to laugh:

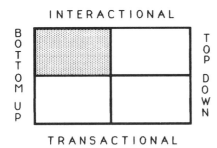

Applications to the design of classroom materials

The kinds of exercises and listening activities used in teaching listening comprehension should reflect the different processes and purposes involved in listening: bottom-up, top-down, interactional, and transactional.

Exercises that involve bottom-up listening

Exercises that require bottom-up processes develop the learner's ability to do the following:

– retain input while it is being processed
– recognize word divisions
– recognize key words in utterances
– recognize key transitions in a discourse
– use knowledge of word-order patterns to identify constituents in utterances
– recognize grammatical relations between key elements in sentences
– recognize the function of word stress in sentences
– recognize the function of intonation in sentences

Such exercises might require the learner to do the following tasks:

– identify the referents of pronouns used in a conversation
– recognize if a sentence is active or passive
– distinguish between sentences containing causative and noncausative verbs
– identify major constituents in a sentence, such as subject and object, verb and adverb
– distinguish between sentences with and without auxiliary verbs
– recognize the use of word stress to mark the information focus of a sentence
– distinguish between sentences containing similar-sounding tenses
– recognize the time reference of a sentence
– distinguish between positive and negative statements
– identify prepositions in rapid speech
– recognize sequence markers
– distinguish between Yes/No and Wh-questions
  (Gore 1979; McLean 1981; Richards, Gordon, and Harper 1987)

These kinds of activities are often more appropriate for learners at a basic level of language proficiency, although the ability to use bottom-up listening strategies is required at all levels of listening. For example, a simple exercise that promotes bottom-up listening might require students to listen to positive and negative statements and choose an appropriate form of agreement.

Students hear:	Students choose an appropriate response:	
That's a nice apartment.	Yes	No
That's not a very nice place to live.	Yes	No
This coffee isn't hot.	Yes	No
This meal is really tasty.	Yes	No

The following exercise practices listening for word stress as a marker of the information focus of a sentence. Students listen to questions that have two possible information focuses and use stress to identify the appropriate focus. For example,

Students hear:	Students check if the person is asking about where or when something is happening:	
Is your *downtown* office open on Saturday?	Where	When
Are the banks open on *Sunday?*	Where	When
Are you going to the *museum* on Tuesday?	Where	When

Exercises that involve top-down listening

Exercises that require top-down processes develop the learner's ability to do the following:

— use key words to construct the schema of a discourse
— construct plans and schema from elements of a discourse
— infer the role of the participants in a situation
— infer the topic of a discourse
— infer the outcome of an event
— infer the cause or effect of an event
— infer unstated details of a situation
— infer the sequence of a series of events
— infer comparisons
— distinguish between literal and figurative meanings
— distinguish between facts and opinions

Exercises that address these goals might require the learner to do tasks like the following:

- listen to part of a conversation and infer the topic of the conversation
- look at pictures and then listen to conversations about the pictures and match them with the pictures
- listen to conversations and identify the setting
- read a list of key points to be covered in a talk and then number them in sequence while listening to the talk
- read information about a topic, then listen to a talk on the topic and check whether the information was mentioned or not
- read one side of a telephone conversation and guess the other speaker's responses; then listen to the telephone conversation
- look at pictures of people speaking and guess what they might be saying or doing; then listen to their actual conversations
- complete a story, then listen to how the story really ended
- guess what news headlines might refer to, then listen to news broadcasts about the events referred to

(Fassman and Tavares 1985; Rost 1986;
Bode and Lee 1987; Richards et al. 1987)

Let us consider listening to news broadcasts and how top-down listening strategies can be the focus of this kind of task. Research on accounts of news events shows that readers and listeners apply specific schemata or scripts to the task. The script "is the catalyst between reader and text that allows a top down approach" (Zuck and Zuck 1984: 147). The script is "a predetermined, stereotyped sequence of actions that defines a well-known situation" (Schank and Abelson 1977: 41) or "a set of stereotypic expectations about content in a given text" (Zuck and Zuck 1984: 148). On reading about or listening to a news broadcast about a political event, such as a change in political leadership, Zuck and Zuck report that some of the obligatory concepts anticipated are:

Who is the new leader?
How did the new leader come to power?
Was the ascension to power anticipated?
What is the reaction of others to this change?
What do we know about the new leader?
What problems will the new leader be facing?

This kind of listening is both top-down and transactional, and can hence be represented as:

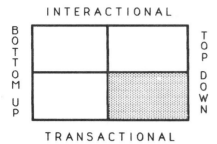

Two quite different approaches to teaching students to listen to news broadcasts are seen in recently published listening materials. In one text, students listen to news items while completing cloze versions of the news transcript. No prelistening activities are included, and no attempt is made to activate or make use of scripts related to the topic of each news item; hence the task focuses primarily on bottom-up processing.

In another text, however, students read headlines and beginnings of stories about news events before they listen to news items. They are asked to guess what the headlines and stories are about. Both of these prelistening tasks help develop a script or schema that students can apply to a subsequent listening task. On first listening to each news item, students complete a simple task in which they identify where each event took place. On a second listening, they indicate whether statements that summarize key information in the news stories are true or false. The tasks focus on identifying key information – students are not required to identify specific words used in the news items. The tasks hence reflect valid purposes in listening to news broadcasts – identifying what happened and where it happened – and allow students to use a top-down rather than a bottom-up approach to listening.

Exercises that involve listening for interactional purposes

Exercises involving interactional purposes seek to develop the learner's ability to do the following:

– recognize when language is being used for interactional purposes
– recognize appropriate moments to make phatic responses in a conversation
– recognize such illocutionary intentions as jokes, compliments, praise
– recognize differences between topics used in small talk and those used as real topics in conversations
– recognize markers of familiarity and social distance between speakers

Exercises that address these goals might require the learner to do tasks such as the following:

– distinguish between conversations that have an interactional and a transactional purpose
– listen to conversations and select suitable polite comments and other phatic responses
– listen to utterances containing compliments or praise and choose suitable responses
– listen to conversations containing small talk and recognize when the speaker is preparing to introduce a real topic
– identify the degree of familiarity between speakers
– distinguish between real invitations and invitations being used to close a conversation

(Lougheed 1985; Richards et al. 1987)

For example, recently a group of teachers who wanted to develop listening activities focusing on listening for interactional purposes collected examples of semiauthentic interactional discourse for use with a group of foreign businessmen planning to visit Canada and the United States. The teachers role-played and recorded social small talk of the kind encountered at cocktail parties. The question then arose of how to use the data obtained as a component in a listening program.

The teachers next examined a commercial text that contained similar kinds of listening samples. This was not particularly helpful, for the text treated casual conversation as if it were an example of transactional discourse – as if the content of such conversation were crucial and every item of the conversation had to be identified:

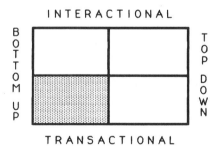

The text required students to listen and complete partial transcripts of conversations, and to answer multiple-choice comprehension questions that tested the content of the conversations in great detail. Such a strong focus on the accurate identification of every word, phrase, and sentence used by the speakers is inappropriate for inter-actional discourse.

The teachers thus opted for a different approach: They developed exercises that first required students to make predictions. For exam-ple, the students were given a setting for a social interaction and a description of the kind of people they would meet. They then had to think of the kinds of questions they might like to ask each person and the kinds of topics they might like to discuss. Following this, they listened to the conversation samples and compared their predic-tions with what was actually talked about, focusing only on the gist of what was said rather than on specific details. Other tasks were developed that focused on how topics were introduced into conver-sations and how people opened and closed conversations. One exer-cise type focused on distinguishing invitations from conversational closings. Students heard closing sequences of conversations and had to identify whether the sequence led to a real invitation or was just a closing sequence. For example:

(1) A: Well, it's been good to see you. I guess I'd better be going now.
　　B: Nice seeing you again, too. We really should get together sometime.
　　A: Let's do that. Well, see you soon.
　　B: Bye.

(2) A: What a surprise it's been seeing you like this!
　　B: Yeah, I'm glad I ran into you. Why don't we have dinner together sometime? How about this weekend?
　　A: That would be nice. I'd like that.

Exercises that involve listening for transactional purposes

Exercises involving transactional functions seek to develop the learner's ability to do the following:

- extract key information from a discourse
- identify specific facts and details in a discourse
- recognize and act on the illocutionary intent of a discourse, such as requests, advice, commands, instructions
- identify the sequence in which a series of events occurred
- carry out tasks as a response to listening

Exercises that address these goals might require the learner to do tasks like the following:

- label the parts of an object from a description of it
- identify the key ideas in a discourse
- follow instructions to assemble an item
- complete a map or picture from an aural description
- write a summary of a talk or conversation
- write down a message delivered aurally
- identify a picture from a description of it
- listen to an advertisement for a job and note down the job requirements
  (Blundell and Stokes 1981; Rost 1986; Richards et al. 1987)

An example of an exercise that involves a transactional purpose for listening would be listening to job announcements on a radio program. To prepare for this task, students might first predict what they expect the requirements for specific jobs to be. Then the students listen to radio announcements about each job and take brief notes. Another example would be listening for information about a travel itinerary. Before listening, students work in groups on planning which cities they would like to visit on a two-week visit to the United States and Canada, and what they would like to do and see in each place. Then they listen to a conversation between a client and a travel agent, during which a visit to North America is planned for the client. Students listen and complete the details of the visit on a form. These kinds of tasks do not require students to attempt to identify every word in what they hear. Rather, the students must attempt to identify key information, a task for which the prelistening activity has given them a script. Both activities are transactional and also involve top-down processing.

An example of a transactional listening purpose involving bottom-up listening would be listening to a description of an event (e.g., a traffic accident) and comparing the information given with a written account of the same event, in order to find out how many differences there were between the two accounts.

Conclusions

In developing classroom activities and materials for teaching listening comprehension, a clear understanding is needed of the nature of top-down and bottom-up approaches to listening and how these processes relate to different kinds of listening purposes. Too often, listening texts require students to adopt a single approach in listening, one that demands a detailed understanding of the content of a discourse and the recognition of every word and structure that occurred in a text. Students should not be required to respond to interactional discourse as if it were being used

65

for a transactional purpose, nor should they be expected to use a bottom-up approach to an aural text if a top-down approach is more appropriate. Ways of using listening passages should be explored that help students employ appropriate listening strategies for particular listening purposes.

Discussion topics and activities

1. Give examples of contexts for listening where bottom-up processing is more important than top-down processing, and vice versa.
2. On page 52 a schema for stories is presented in the form of a set of questions a listener might use in listening to a story. Prepare similar schemas by developing specific questions that someone might use in listening to a report of:
   a) a visit to the dentist
   b) a domestic argument
   c) a traffic accident
   d) a political crisis
3. Can you expand the list of examples of top-down processes given on page 52?
4. Give examples of situations where language use is primarily:
   a) transactional
   b) interactional
   c) a mixture of both
5. Critique the list of exercise types dealing with the four dimensions of listening (pp. 59–65). Can you suggest other exercise types that would address these listening processes?
6. Record an example of language being used for (a) transactional purposes and (b) interactional purposes. Examine each example and consider the kinds of demands it makes on a listener in terms of bottom-up and top-down processing.
7. Examine a second or foreign language listening text. What is its focus? What kinds of listening situations, purposes, and skills does it address? What kinds of exercise types and activities does it use? How appropriate are they to the focus?
8. Choose a sample of authentic listening material (either the material you recorded in question 6 or something else) that would be appropriate for use in a second language listening class. Plan a lesson around the tape or video material, and develop suitable listening exercises and activities for use with it.

4 Conversationally speaking: approaches to the teaching of conversation

The "conversation class" is something of an enigma in language teaching. In some language programs it is an opportunity for untrained native speakers to get students to talk for the duration of a class period, using whatever resources and techniques the teacher can think of. In language programs where trained language teachers are available, they are often left to their own resources and encouraged to dip into whatever materials they choose in order to provide practice in both "accuracy" and "fluency." Consequently the content of conversation classes varies widely. In one class, the teacher's primary emphasis might be on problem solving. Students work on communication games and tasks in pairs or small groups with relatively little direct teacher input. In another class, the teacher might have a more active role, employing grammar and pronunciation drills and structured oral tasks. A third teacher may use the conversation class as an opportunity for unstructured free discussion, while in another class the teacher might have students work on situational dialogues such as "At the bank" and "At the supermarket."

Part of the difficulty in deciding what to do in the conversation class is due to the nature of conversation itself. What is conversation and what is involved in producing fluent, appropriate, and intelligible conversation? Can conversation be taught or is it something that is acquired simply by doing it? What principles can be used in planning a conversation program and in developing classroom activities and materials? These questions are addressed in this chapter by first examining the nature of conversation, and then considering the implications for planning an approach to the teaching of conversation.

The nature of conversation

Conversation is a multifaceted activity. In order to appreciate the complex nature of conversation and conversational fluency, some of the most important dimensions of conversation are examined here: the purposes of conversation, turn-taking, topics, repair, formal features of conversation, and the notion of fluency.

Purposes of conversation

Conversations serve a variety of purposes. As was illustrated in Chapter 3, two different kinds of conversational interaction can be distinguished – those in which the primary focus is on the exchange of information (the transactional function of conversation), and those in which the primary purpose is to establish and maintain social relations (the interactional function of conversation) (Brown and Yule 1983). In transactional uses of conversation the primary focus is on the message, whereas interactional uses of conversation focus primarily on the social needs of the participants. Approaches to the teaching of both conversation and listening comprehension are fundamentally affected by whether the primary purposes involved are transactional or interactional.

Conversation also reflects the rules and procedures that govern face-to-face encounters, as well as the constraints that derive from the use of spoken language. This is seen in the nature of turns, the role of topics, how speakers repair trouble spots, as well as the syntax and register of conversational discourse.

Turn-taking

Conversation is a collaborative process. A speaker does not say everything he or she wants to say in a single utterance. Conversations progress as a series of "turns"; at any moment, the speaker may become the listener. Basic to the management of the collaborative process in conversation is the turn-taking system.

A basic rule of conversation is that only one person speaks at a time, and in North American settings participants work to ensure that talk is continuous. Silence or long pauses are considered awkward and embarrassing, even though in other cultures this is not the case. Successful management and control of the turn-taking system in conversation involves control of a number of strategies (Wardhaugh 1985).

Strategies for taking a turn. These involve ways of entering into a conversation or taking over the role of speaker, and include

- using interjections to signal a request for a turn, such as "Mm-hmm," "Yeah," and rising intonation
- using facial or other gestures to indicate a wish to take a turn
- accepting a turn offered by another speaker by responding to a question or by providing the second part of an adjacency pair (e.g., expressing thanks in response to a compliment)
- completing or adding to something said by the speaker

Strategies for holding a turn. These involve indicating that one has more to say – for example, through intonation or by using expressions to suggest continuity, such as "First," "Another thing," "Then."

Strategies for relinquishing the turn. These are devices used to bring the other person(s) into the conversation, and include

- using adjacency pairs, requiring the other person to provide the sequence, such as with the adjacency pair challenge–denial:
  A: You look tired.
  B: I feel fine.
- using phonological signals, such as slowing down the final syllables of an utterance and increasing the pitch change to signal completion of the turn
- pausing to provide an opportunity for someone to take up the turn
- using a facial or bodily gesture to signal that a turn is finished

Participants in conversation are involved in ongoing evaluation of each other's utterances to judge appropriate places to take up the turn to talk. As Slade (1986: 79) observes:

Turntaking and turn assignment in conversation can be difficult for a second language speaker. A learner who mistimes his entry into conversation or who is unfamiliar with the correct formulae can give the impression of being "pushy" or, conversely, over-reticent.

In addition to use of turn-taking strategies, speakers are required to use both short and long turns (Brown and Yule 1983). A short turn consists of one or two utterances:

A: Did you like the movie?
B: It was all right.
A: Who was in it?
B: Shelley Long.

A long turn might be required for a speaker to explain an opinion, describe something, or tell a joke or a story. For example, the following speaker is recounting an encounter with a cockroach during an examination.

We were sitting for our analytical chemistry exam and it was the final exam. And they have sort of like bench desks where there's three to a bench normally and they had the middle seat empty – and two sat either side, and I was sitting there and I thought, "Geez I can feel something on my foot." And I thought, "No, no, don't worry about it," you know, "What on earth is this chemical equation?" and I'm trying to think. But there's something on my foot and I looked down and there was this cockroach like – and I just screamed and jumped up on the chair. (Slade 1986: 86)

The inability to take up long turns in conversation is a feature of many second language speakers, who keep to short turns and appear to be less than collaborative conversational partners.

The role of topics[1]

The way topics are selected for discussion within conversation and the strategies speakers use to introduce, develop, or change topics within conversations constitute another important dimension of conversational management. For example, coherent conversation respects norms concerning the choice of topics. Questions concerning one's age, salary, and marital status may be appropriate on first encounters in some cultures, but not in others. Coulthard (1977: 75–6) comments:

An initial question is what sort of things can and do form topics in conversation? Some topics are not relevant to particular conversations...and the suitability of other topics depends on the person one is talking to. We experience, see, hear about events all the time...Some are tellable to everyone, some have a restricted audience, some must be told immediately, and some can wait and still retain their interest.

Part of the structure of conversational openings has to do with the positioning of topics within the conversation, as Schegloff and Sacks (1973) point out. The participants select a topic as first topic through a process of negotiation. The first topic, however, may be held back until the conversation develops to a point where it can be appropriately introduced. For example, a conversation may open:

A: What's up?
B: Not much. What's up with you?
A: Nothing.

Later, after possible preambles, one of the participants may go on to introduce a topic such as a job offer, which could have been given as a direct response to "What's up?". As Goffman points out, conversationalists might want to "talk past" some topics initially, waiting until a much later time to introduce a sensitive issue, "all of which management requires some understanding of issues such as delicacy"(Goffman 1976: 268). Schegloff and Sacks have also pointed out that in telephone conversations there is often a preamble to the first topic that offers the possibility of closing the conversation, should the other speaker so desire, such as "Did I wake you up?" or "Are you busy?", which if declined becomes a presequence for topic talk.

Winskowski (1977, 1978) refers to topicalizing behavior, by which is meant bringing up topics, responding to other people's topics, mention-

1 This section is adapted from Richards and Schmidt (1983).

ing something, avoiding the mention of something, carrying the discussion one step further, and so on – the creating of topic in the activity. With this focus on topic as process, topic behavior can often be seen to consist of rounds of topical turns that are reciprocally addressed and replied to, as in the following example:

A: Oh nothing, we're just cleaning up. We had dinner. What's new?
B: Nothing much. I still got a cold.
A: Oh, has it improved at all, hopefully?
B: Yeah, it's gotten better, it's gotten better. It'll be all right
tomorrow. It better because I'm going out tomorrow.

(Winskowski 1977: 86)

Hatch (1978) emphasizes that second language learners need a wide range of topics at their disposal. Initially, learners may depend on "canned topics." Although they may get by with their ability to answer questions about recurring topics, such as how long they have been in the country, their occupation, and family, learners need practice in introducing new topics into conversation in order to move beyond this stage.

They should practice nominating topics about which they are prepared to speak. They should do lots of listening comprehension for topic nominations of native speakers. They should practice predicting questions for a large number of topics...They should be taught...elicitation devices...to get topic clarification. That is, they should practice saying "huh," echoing parts of sentences they do not understand in order to get the rest of it recycled again, "pardon me, excuse me, I didn't understand etc." Nothing stops the opportunity to carry on a conversation quicker than silence or the use of "yes" and head-nodding when the learner does not understand. (Hatch 1978: 434)

Learners also need to be able to follow the flow of a topic through conversation. Knowledge of the real world in the form of schema knowledge is one source of information the learner can make use of, predicting and anticipating questions and the direction of conversation for certain topics.

Repair

Repair refers to efforts by both parties in conversation to correct problems that arise. Van Lier (1988: 180–2) emphasizes that discourse involves

continuous adjustment between speakers and hearers obliged to operate in a code which gives them problems. This adjustment-in-interaction may be crucial to language development, for it leads to noticing discrepancies between what is said and what is heard, and to a resolution of these discrepancies...

Repairing, as one of the mechanisms of feedback ... is likely to be an important variable in language learning. Although it is not a sufficient condition, we may safely assume that it is a necessary condition.

Repairs may be initiated by either the speaker (*self-repairs*) or the hearer (*other repairs*). The second language learner may also request clarification from a native speaker (NS) when misunderstanding occurs. *Echoing* is one technique that is used, when the nonnative speaker (NNS) repeats a word or phrase that is not understood and the conversational partner explains it or replaces it with an easier item.

NS: We're going mountaineering tomorrow.
NNS: Mountain ... ee ... ?
NS: Mountaineering. You know, to climb up the mountain.

Another response to a request for repair involves topic fronting, as in the following example:

NS: Do you come from a big family?
NNS: Uhh?
NS: Your family. Is it big? Do you have lots of brothers and sisters?

Formal features of conversation

Conversational discourse is also recognized by formal features, which distinguish it from written discourse (see Chapter 6).

SYNTAX

Written language exhibits a different syntax from spoken discourse. In the written mode, clauses are linked in complex ways, with a main clause often followed by or linked to subordinate clauses. Rules of intra- and intersentential relations serve to link repeated and coreferential constituents. This is not possible in spoken discourse. Brown and Yule (1983: 4) observe:

Most spoken language consists of paratactic (unsubordinated) phrases which are marked as related to each other, not so much by the syntax as by the way the speaker says them. The speaker uses the resources of pausing and rhythm and, to a lesser extent, intonation, to mark out for the listener which parts of his speech need to be co-interpreted.

Similarly, Syder (1983: 32) notes:

Normal procedure in spontaneous connected discourse is for the speaker to package his thoughts into a series of relatively complete and independent clauses. All the syntactic and semantic elements needed to understand the clause are present in the clause, and there is minimal cross referencing to other clauses required of the hearer.

Bygate concludes (1987: 62–3):

The learner engaged in oral communication is more likely to be working with small chunks than any other user of language. This is because, in addition to the fragmentary nature of oral discourse, the learner's processing capacity is limited.

Bygate notes that in conversation, speakers tend to avoid complex noun groups containing a series of adjectives (e.g., "an elegant new red two-door Italian sports car") and instead spread adjectives out over several clauses. As a result, spoken language is less dense than written language. Bygate gives an example of a second language learner describing a picture:

OK – in this picture in picture – er – number 1 – I can see er a little girl – who probably – is inside – her house – er who is playing – with a bear – this bear – it has a brown colour and – the little girl is sitting – in the – in the stairs of her house – this house is very nice – it has rugs – it has brown rugs – mm – it has waste basket. (Bygate 1987: 16)

STYLES OF SPEAKING

An important dimension of conversation is using a style of speaking that is appropriate to the particular circumstances. Different styles of speaking reflect the roles, age, sex, and status of participants in interactions. Consider the various ways in which it is possible to ask someone the time, and the different social meanings that are communicated by these differences:

Got the time?
I guess it must be quite late now – is it?
What's the time?
Do you have the time?
Would you know what time it is?
Could I trouble you for the time?

Lexical, phonological, and grammatical changes may be involved in producing a suitable style of speaking, as the following alternatives illustrate:

Have you seen the boss? / Have you seen the manager?   (lexical)
Whachadoin'? / What are you doing?   (phonological)
Seen Joe lately? / Have you seen Joe lately?   (grammatical)

Different speech styles reflect perceptions of the social roles of the participants in a speech event. However, if the speaker and hearer are judged to be of more or less equal status, a casual speech style is appropriate that stresses affiliation and solidarity. If the participants are perceived as being of uneven power or status, a more formal speech style is appropriate, one that marks the dominance of one speaker over the other. Successful management of speech styles creates the sense of politeness that is essential for harmonious social relations (Brown and Levinson 1978).

Brown and Yule (1983) point out that speech in a casual conversational style is peppered with general nonspecific words and phrases (e.g., the *thing* is, it's *sort* of..., the *kind of thing, you know,* it's a *bit* like...,) and with interactive expressions (*well, oh, mm, really, actually, yes, geez*). This is well illustrated in an extract from Svartik and Quirk's *A Corpus of English Conversation* (cited in Wardaugh 1985: 202–3). The two speakers are male academics discussing the use of diaries in language research.

A: I don't know whether you have talked with Hilary about the diary situation
B: Well she has been explaining to me rather in more general terms, what you are sort of doing and
A: What it was all about, yes.
B: I gather you've been at it for nine years.
A: By golly that's true. Yes, yes, it's not a long time of course, in this sort of work, you know.
B: Well no, but it's quite a long time by any standards.
A: Yes, suppose so.
B: She told me what you did, and we decided we were both a bit out of date compared with the present day students and
A: Well I suppose that that's true

The ability to produce this kind of casual conversational language as well as to produce language appropriate for more formal encounters is an essential skill for second language learners.

CONVERSATIONAL ROUTINES

Another characteristic of conversational discourse is the use of fixed expressions or "routines," which often have specific functions in conversation. Wardhaugh (1985: 74) observes:

There are routines to help people establish themselves in certain positions: routines for taking off and hanging up coats; arrangements concerning where one is to sit or stand at a party or in a meeting; offers of hospitality; and so on. There are routines for beginnings and endings of conversations, for leading into topics, and for moving away from one topic to another. And there are routines for breaking up conversations, for leaving a party, and for dissolving a gathering...It is difficult...to imagine how life could be lived without some routines.

Consider the following routines. Where might they occur? What might be their function within those situations?

This one's on me.	Guess I'll be making a move.
I don't believe a word of it.	I see what you mean.
I don't get the point.	Let me think about it.
You look great today.	Just looking, thanks.
What will you have to drink?	I'll be with you in a minute.
Nearly time. Got everything?	It doesn't matter.
Check please!	No harm done.
After you.	

Pawley and Syder (1983) suggest that native speakers have a repertoire of thousands of routines like these, and their use in appropriate situations creates conversational discourse that sounds natural and nativelike. Conversational routines typically have to be learned and used as fixed expressions, but at the same time, speakers must be aware that they cannot be used indiscriminately, to avoid exchanges such as the following:

A: Thanks for the meal.   A: Terry's father died.
B: It doesn't matter.   B: What a nuisance.

The concept of fluency

The overall goal of a second language learner is to produce fluent speech; however, the notion of fluency is difficult to pin down. The European Threshold Level Project (Van Ek 1977; Van Ek and Alexander 1980), for example, describes oral fluency in terms of "reasonable speech: with sufficient precision: with reasonable correctness (grammatically, lexically, phonologically)." Fillmore (1979: 93) describes fluency in terms of "the ability to fill time with talk ... the ability to talk in coherent, reasoned and 'semantically dense' sentences" showing "a mastery of the semantic and syntactic resources of the language"; "the ability to have appropriate things to say in a wide range of contexts"; and the ability to "be creative and imaginative ... in language use." Hieke (1985: 140) states that "fluent speech is the cumulative result of dozens of different kinds of processes" with both quantitative and qualitative dimensions. Although fluency is a fuzzy concept, it is not an unimportant one.

The concept of fluency reflects the assumption that speakers set out to produce discourse that is comprehensible, easy to follow, and free from errors and breakdowns in communication, though this goal is often not met due to processing and production demands. "The prime objective of the speaker is the generation of maximally acceptable speech in both content and form and a concomitant minimization of errors by the time an utterance has been articulated" (Hieke 1981: 150). Hieke proposes three conversational "maxims" that motivate the speaker:

1. Be Error-Free (phonology and syntax)
2. Be Intelligible (semantics, lexicon, logic, stylistics, and rhetoric)
3. Be in Control of the Communication Channel (fluency, and in dyadic speech, also turn taking).

(1981: 151)

Accuracy (including control of grammar and pronunciation) is here seen as a *component* of fluency, rather than as an independent dimension of conversational skill. The kind of discourse speakers produce and the degree of fluency they achieve, however, depend upon the task the speaker is attempting and the context for communication (i.e., whether the speech situation involves face-to-face conversation, whether the speaker is taking part in an interview or a discussion, or whether the speaker is involved in telling a story, giving a description, or replying to a question).

For some tasks, such as telling a story, the speaker may have access to available plans or schemas that reduce planning time and effort. The result may be that the discourse produced is qualitatively different from discourse produced during spontaneous interaction. It may be less hesitant, and the speaker may be able to plan larger units of discourse than are found in unplanned conversational interaction. Holmes (1984) found that the types of clauses and pauses occurring in storytelling tasks differed from those found in spontaneous interaction. Storytelling tasks "allowed subjects to construct more integrated utterances, which have been largely thought out and organized prior to their expression. The utterances are more *planned,* compared with the relatively unplanned discourse of spontaneous speech, which lacks much forethought and preparation" (Holmes 1984: 129).

Within a particular task type, however, such as storytelling, there may be variation between a hesitant cycle and a more fluent cycle, the latter marked by a faster rate of speech and fewer hesitations. Clark and Clark suggest that as the speaker begins a new idea, more detailed planning is required, resulting in more hesitant speech. Once the speaker gets further into the idea or topic, however, planning and execution require less effort. "Each new section in discourse takes special global planning in the beginning, and this reveals itself in a hesitant output. As the section proceeds, the global plan becomes complete, there is less need to hesitate, and the result is a fluent output" (Clark and Clark 1977: 272).

Approaches to the teaching of conversation

Currently there are two major approaches to the teaching of conversation in second language programs. One is an indirect approach, in which conversational competence is seen as the product of engaging learners in conversational interaction. The second, a more direct approach, involves planning a conversation program around the specific microskills, strategies, and processes that are involved in fluent conversation.

The indirect approach: teaching conversation through interactive tasks

The justification for a task-based approach to the teaching of conversation comes from second language acquisition (SLA) research. SLA researchers (e.g., Hatch 1978) have argued that learners acquire language through conversation. In using conversation to interact with others, learners gradually acquire the competence that underlies the ability to use language. Hatch (1978: 404) puts the position in this way: "One learns how to do conversation, one learns how to interact verbally, and out of this interaction syntactic structures are developed."

Studies of conversational interaction have revealed a great deal about the nature of nonnative speaker-to-native speaker conversational interaction, clarifying its role in second language learning. For example, the discourse found in conversation between nonnative speakers and native speakers is usually syntactically less complex than NS–NS discourse, with a higher frequency of more regular grammatical structures and vocabulary. This should make comprehension easier for the nonnative speaker. There are characteristic patterns of question use. Questions are more frequent than statements, drawing the nonnative speaker into conversation and allowing the native speaker to check comprehension at the same time. Native speakers ask more Yes/No questions than Wh-questions, presumably because Yes/No questions are easier to answer. Questions may also contain their own answers (e.g., "Are you working or are you on vacation?"), providing the nonnative speaker with a model for the expected answer. These kinds of conversational modifications are believed to assist the second language learner's language development. Pica comments,

In sum, what enables learners to move beyond their current interlanguage receptive and expressive capacities when they need to understand unfamiliar linguistic input or when required to produce a comprehensible message are opportunities to modify and restructure their interaction with their interlocutor until mutual comprehension is reached. (1987: 8)

Through the kinds of linguistic and interactional modifications and adjustments learners receive when engaged in conversation, the grammatical structure of the language is displayed more clearly and made more accessible. Comprehension is assisted and the learner is able to experiment with the internal mechanisms of the language. As a direct result of this process, SLA researchers argue, linguistic competence gradually emerges.

The conclusion drawn from this view of the relationship between conversation and second language learning is that the conversation class should primarily provide opportunities for learners to engage in natural interaction through the use of communicative tasks and activities. It is not necessary (or even possible) to *teach* conversation in any real sense; all that is needed is provision of opportunities for learners to engage in conversational interaction. In practical terms, this leads to the use of pair-work and group-work activities that require learner-to-learner interaction. Tasks most likely to bring this about involve information sharing and negotiation of meaning (Johnson 1982). The focus is on using language to complete a task, rather than on practicing language for its own sake. According to Long and Porter (1985: 207), "Provided careful attention is paid to the structure of tasks students work on together, the negotiation work possible in group work makes it an attractive alternative to the teacher-led, 'lockstep' mode, and a viable classroom substitute for individual conversations with native speakers."

However, there are obvious limitations to an exclusively task-based approach to teaching conversation. Higgs and Clifford, for example, report experience with foreign language teaching programs in the U.S. government and elsewhere:

In programs that have as curricular goals an early emphasis on unstructured communication activities – minimizing, or excluding entirely, considerations of grammatical accuracy – it is possible in a fairly short time...to provide students with a relatively large vocabulary and a high degree of fluency... These same data suggest that the premature immersion of a student into an unstructured or "free" conversational setting before certain fundamental linguistic structures are more or less in place is not done without cost. There appears to be a real danger of leading the students too rapidly into the "creative aspects of language use," in that if successful communication is encouraged and rewarded for its own sake, the effect seems to be one of rewarding at the same time the *incorrect* communication strategies seized upon in attempting to deal with the communication strategies presented. (Higgs and Clifford 1982: 73–4)

Although Higgs and Clifford offer no data to substantiate this claim, Schmidt and Frota (1986: 281), describing a case study of Schmidt's own acquisition of Portuguese through "immersion," similarly report that "interaction with native speakers provided input that sometimes leads to language learning, but interaction guaranteed neither grammaticality nor idiomaticity." Schmidt found that his Portuguese was deficient both with respect to grammar and appropriateness, and that further interaction with native speakers did not appear to remedy this. Similarly, in a study of ESL learners interacting with each other on communicative tasks, Porter (1986) found that learners often produced inappropriate forms. In learner-to-learner communication, 20% of forms produced were grammatically faulty (not including errors of pronunciation). Others were sociolinguistically inappropriate, such as inappropriate ways of expressing opinions, agreement, and disagreement. "These findings... suggest that only native speakers (or perhaps very advanced nonnative speakers) can provide truly appropriate input that will build sociolinguistic competence" (Porter 1986: 218). Alternatively, the study suggests that although communicative tasks may be a necessary component of a conversation program, they are not a sufficient component.

Another limitation of a task-based approach to teaching conversation relates to the kind of interaction such tasks typically involve. An examination of the communicative activities commonly employed in task-based teaching (e.g., Klippel 1984; Pattison 1987) reveals that they typically deal only with the transactional uses of language. Communication and pair-work activities often focus on using conversation to convey information, to negotiate meaning, or to complete a task but ignore the use of conversation to create social interaction and social relations. Interactional uses of conversation are very different in both form and function from the kinds of transactional language found in task-oriented communication, and should have a central place in a conversation program. In order to ensure that this happens, a direct attempt to teach strategies for conversational interaction is also needed.

Direct approaches: teaching strategies for casual conversation

A direct approach to teaching conversation is one that focuses explicitly on the processes and strategies involved in casual conversation. The program hence addresses directly such aspects of conversation as strategies for turn-taking, topic control, and repair; conversational routines; fluency; pronunciation; and differences between formal and casual conversational styles. Designing such a program begins with the preparation of goals, samples of which are:

– How to use conversation for both transactional and interactional purposes
– How to produce both short and long turns in conversation
– Strategies for managing turn-taking in conversation, including taking a turn, holding a turn, and relinquishing a turn
– Strategies for opening and closing conversations
– How to initiate and respond to talk on a broad range of topics, and how to develop and maintain talk on these topics
– How to use both a casual style of speaking and a neutral or more formal style
– How to use conversation in different social settings and for different

TABLE 4.1. THE USE OF OBJECTIVES IN PROGRAM PLANNING

ORAL INTERACTION	Family Identification	Social Contacts	Banking Services	Employment	Health	Housing	The Law	Entertainment	Postal Services	Safety	Shopping	Transport	Child Care
– use appropriately conversational formula for greetings, salutations, leave taking, indicating lack of comprehension, requesting, repetition, etc.													
– respond to requests for factual information													
– ask for factual information													
– offer and ask for help													
– indicate likes and dislikes													
– state basic conceptual meanings, e.g. numbers, time, dates, quantity, location, etc.													
– ask about likes and dislikes													
– describe entities, objects or individuals													
– maintain simple conversation on familiar topic													
– make arrangements involving time/location													
– conduct simple telephone transaction on familiar topic													
– respond to a number of related questions for advice or opinion													
– ask a number of related questions to solicit advice or opinion													
– express agreement and disagreement													
– give a sequence of oral instructions/directions													
– respond to requests for clarification													
– describe a sequence of events													

Reprinted with permission from Nunan (1985: 29).

kinds of social encounters, such as on the telephone, at informal and formal social gatherings
- Strategies for repairing trouble spots in conversation, including communication breakdown and comprehension problems
- How to maintain fluency in conversation, through avoiding excessive pausing, breakdowns, and errors of grammar or pronunciation
- How to produce talk in a conversational mode, using a conversational register and syntax
- How to use conversational fillers and small talk
- How to use conversational routines

In program planning and development, each goal can be described in more detail as an *objective* or set of objectives, according to the level of language proficiency the program addresses and the specific needs of the learners. For example Nunan (1985) describes the use of objectives grids in program planning. These allow general objectives for different aspects of oral skill to be cross-referenced to different topic areas (Table 4.1). Each objective can be specified in more detail by describing the kind of interaction to be taught and the performance level that is expected. For example:

Level:	basic
Objective:	respond to requests for factual information
Content area:	personal and family identification
Specific objective:	the learner will provide personal information in a simulated interview with a government official
Standards:	responses to be comprehensible to someone used to dealing with second language learners
Evaluation:	the student will perform in a simulated interview with a teacher from another class

(Nunan 1985: 24)

A related approach is given in Omaggio (1986), who provides an example of a curriculum planning guide for speaking skills at the intermediate level (see Appendix).

Whatever approach to goal and syllabus specification is adopted (see Chapter 1 for discussion of different options), recognition of these kinds of goals is an essential starting point in developing an effective conversation program, and provides a basis for the design and selection of classroom activities and materials.

Classroom activities and materials

A number of attempts have been made to classify exercises and activity types according to the aspects of conversational management and production they focus on (e.g., Littlewood 1981; Harmer 1983). Littlewood (1981), for example, distinguishes four main kinds of activities:

Precommunicative activities *Communicative activities*
Structural activities   Functional communicative activities
Quasi-communicative activities Social-interactional activities

Precommunicative activities are those that deal with controlled practice of formal aspects of conversation, and include drills, dialogues, and other exercises where little learner input is required. The distinction between functional communicative activities and social-interactional activities is similar to Brown and Yule's distinction between transactional and interactional uses of conversation.

A wide variety of exercise types and classroom materials are available for teaching different aspects of conversation. There are materials that deal both with the global dimensions of conversation as well as specific aspects of conversational management. Texts such as *Person to Person* (Richards and Bycina 1984), *Functions of American English* (Jones and von Baeyer 1983), and *English Firsthand* (Helgesen, Brown, and Mandeville 1987), for example, take the global approach. Others deal with particular conversation skills. *Gambits* (Keller and Taba-Warner 1976), for example, deals with strategies for opening and closing conversations as well as with specific conversational routines used in managing turn-taking and topics. Task-based activities such as those described in Brown and Yule (1983) deal with transactional uses of language and the production of longer turns. Ur (1981) deals with discussion skills; Holden (1981), Livingstone (1983), and Jones (1983) with role play and simulations; and Klippel (1984) and Pattison (1987) with communication activities.

In developing classroom materials and activities, it is necessary to monitor their use in the classroom in order to determine which aspects of conversation they practice. In Richards (1985), this approach is described in relation to the development and use of role-play activities. In developing a set of role-play materials for use with a class of intermediate-level ESL learners, a range of topics and transactions was first selected covering both transactional and interactional uses of conversation. Role-play activities were then planned around each topic based on the following design format:

1. Learners first take part in a preliminary activity that introduces the topic and the situation, and provides some background information. Such activities include brainstorming, ranking exercises, and problem-solving tasks. For example, as preparation for a role play on renting an apartment, students first interview each other about their accommodation and living arrangements. They also perform a rank-

ing task in which they list the things that would most influence their choice of an apartment. The focus is on thinking about a topic, generating vocabulary and related language, and developing expectations about the topic. This activity prepares learners for a role-play task by establishing a schema for the situation.

2. Students then practice a dialogue on the topic (e.g., a conversation between a person looking for an apartment and a landlord). This serves to model the kind of transaction the learner will have to perform in the role-play task, and provides examples of the kind of language that could be used to carry out the transaction.

3. Learners perform a role play, using role cards. Students practice the role play several times, in different roles and with different partners. For example:

Student A (Caller)
You want to rent an apartment. You saw this advertisement in the newspaper.

George Street
Large modern apartment
Only $600 a month
Tel. 789–6445

Call to find out more about the apartment. Ask about these things:

the bedrooms	the neighborhood
the view	nearby transportation
the furniture	nearby shopping
the floor it's on	

Ask anything else you want to know.
Find out when you can come and see it.

Student B (Landlord)
You have an apartment to rent. You placed this advertisement in the newspaper.

George Street
Large modern apartment
Only $600 a month
Tel. 789–6445

A person telephones to ask about the apartment. Answer the person's questions. (See Richards and Hull 1987.)

4. Learners then listen to recordings of native speakers performing the same role play from the same role-play cues. By having learners listen to NS versions of the tasks they have just practiced, students are able to compare differences between the ways they expressed particular functions and meanings and the ways native speakers performed. Although the NS versions are more complex than the student versions, they are comprehensible because of the preparatory activities

83

the students have completed, and they can be used for follow-up and feedback activities.
5. Feedback and follow-up activities consist of listening for specific conversational and grammatical forms (idioms, routines, structures) used by the native speakers in their versions of the role plays, as well as listening for meaning.

In order to determine the kinds of conversational practice the role-play tasks provided, data were collected on the type of conversational interaction and discourse students produced when completing the role-play tasks (Richards 1985b; Hull 1986). Among the features of conversational interaction students were found to employ were repairs, requests for clarification, short and long turns, openings and closings, topicalization behavior including strategies for topic nomination and topic change, use of polite forms, and politeness strategies. Repairs showed that students were monitoring their production for vocabulary, grammar, and appropriateness.

Conclusions

In planning a conversation program, an understanding of the nature of conversation and conversational interaction is a necessary starting point. Two complementary approaches to the teaching of conversation are currently advocated and employed in program development and methodology: an indirect approach, which focuses on using communicative activities to generate conversational interaction, and a direct approach, which addresses specific aspects of conversational management. A balance of both approaches would seem to be the most appropriate methodological option. Although communicative tasks that focus on the transactional uses of conversation provide useful language learning opportunities, methodology should also address the nature of casual conversation and conversational fluency, particularly turn-taking strategies, topic behavior, appropriate styles of speaking, conversational syntax, and conversational routines. Instructional materials and activities should be planned to focus on these aspects of casual conversation, and monitored to determine their effectiveness in promoting conversational fluency.

Discussion topics and activities

1. Interview several teachers of conversation skills. What do they see the primary purpose of a conversation class to be? What aspects of

conversation do they spend most time on in class? What kinds of activities do they use and how often? What do they see the greatest difficulties in teaching a conversation class to be?

2. Try to observe (or overhear) a casual conversation between a native speaker and a nonnative speaker, or between two nonnative speakers. What kinds of turn-taking strategies do the nonnative speakers use?

3. Discuss the notions of accuracy and fluency. Do you agree that accuracy is a component of fluency, rather than a separate dimension? How can accuracy be addressed in a conversation program?

4. Examine the list of goals for a conversation program on pages 79–81. What additions or deletions would you want to make to the list?

5. Choose two other skills listed by Nunan in Table 4.1. Prepare statements of objectives for each skill, using the format given by Nunan shown on page 81.

6. Choose a conversational task or activity from a second language text and try it out (either with classmates or with second language learners). Record the students doing the activity. Then listen to the recording and determine which aspects of conversational management the activity improves. Does the activity focus primarily on transactional or interactional skills? Could the design of the activity be improved?

7. Plan and try out classroom activities that focus on (a) turn-taking, (b) conversational routines, and (c) differences between formal and informal styles.

Appendix

The following is an intermediate-level curricular planning guide for speaking skills from Omaggio (1986).

Level: Intermediate
Skill: Speaking

Content

Everyday survival topics such as ...
Personal/biographical information
Restaurant/foods
Asking/giving directions
Activities/hobbies
Transportation
Talking on phone
Lodging/living quarters
Money matters
Health matters
Post office
Numbers 1–1000
Customs
Shopping/making purchases
Courtesy/social requirements
  such as ...
Greetings/introductions
Making appointments
Making meeting arrangements
Accepting/refusing invitations
Polite, formulaic expressions

Functions

Can create with the language
Can make up own sentences not
  limited to very familiar or
  memorized material
Can participate in short
  conversations
Can ask and answer questions
Can get into, through, and out of a
  simple survival situation
Can transfer current learned material
  to new situations/contexts

Techniques

Personalized questions
Personalized completions
Personalized true/false
Sentence builders
Dialogue/story adaptation
Create a story with visuals
Chain stories
Describing objects/processes
Surveys and polls
Conversation cards
Paired interviews
Social interaction activities
Group consensus/problem solving
Storytelling
Forced choice
Role plays
Slash sentences
Elaboration
Giving definitions
Guided description/narration
Asking related questions
Logical questions

Accuracy

Comprehensible to native speakers
  used to dealing with target-
  language learners
Some accuracy in basic structures
Uses short sentences
Minimal sociolinguistic knowledge in
  evidence
Very basic vocabulary related to
  content areas listed

Reprinted with permission from A. Omaggio, *Teaching Language in Context*, p. 181, © 1986 by Heinle & Heinle, Boston.

5 A profile of an effective reading teacher

The field of second and foreign language reading has been revitalized in recent years by changes in our understanding of the nature of the reading process. On the one hand, reading theory and research has contributed notions such as top-down and bottom-up processing. Reading is no longer viewed as a process of decoding, but rather as an integration of top-down processes that utilize background knowledge and schema, as well as bottom-up processes that are primarily text or data driven (Carrell, Devine, and Eskey 1988). In addition, researchers have focused on readers themselves and have sought to identify the strategies employed by successful readers as they interact with a text during reading (see Chapter 2). Using think-aloud and introspective/retrospective research techniques, students perform reading tasks and verbalize their thought processes, reflecting upon the cognitive strategies and heuristics they employ when dealing with different kinds of reading problems (Hosenfeld 1984).

The second or foreign language reading teacher who understands the differences between top-down and bottom-up processing and the role played by schema and background knowledge in reading will look for classroom strategies that encourage second language readers to use an appropriate combination of processing strategies when they approach a text. Likewise a familiarity with differences between effective and ineffective reading strategies can help the teacher look for effective reading behaviors in learners, encourage wider use of these strategies, and be on the lookout for learners using less effective strategies.

Missing in the growing literature on second and foreign language reading, however, is consideration of teachers themselves and what it is that effective teachers do in the reading classroom. What teaching and learning behaviors can an observer expect to see in the classroom of a good reading teacher? In preparing student teachers for classroom observations, it is useful for them to consider this question *before* they begin observing reading classes, as a way of creating a schema for their observations. When students do an exercise of this kind, however, they should restrict their speculations to those behaviors and qualities that apply to a *reading* class, as opposed to any well-taught second language class. Hence general teaching characteristics, such as good classroom management skills, good pacing, and evidence of careful preparation of the lesson, should be excluded from consideration. The reader of this chapter is invited at this juncture to pause and perform such an exercise, and to generate a short list of characteristics that one would expect to observe in a good second language reading class.

The notion of good or effective teaching is not a fashionable one in current conceptualizations of second language teaching or learning. Second language acquisition research has virtually excluded the teacher as a participant in the process of second language teaching. As Van Lier (1988: 23) observes, "We thus have the curious situation that most second-language acquisition theorizing ignores the L2 classroom as a relevant source of data and as a relevant place to apply findings." While classroom-based research has been more willing to acknowledge the teacher's presence in the classroom, the kinds of teaching behaviors that are typically investigated are restricted to those that are readily quantifiable or that can be described in units of linguistic analysis. Such research reflects a *quantitative approach* to the study of teaching. Hence much classroom research is reduced to frequency counts of moves and transactions, interaction patterns, question types, and the like. While this approach is necessary if one is primarily interested in the linguistic or discoursal structure of lessons (Cazden 1987), other approaches are needed in order to broaden our understanding of the nature of classrooms and of good teaching. This often necessitates more of a *qualitative approach* – that is, one that looks at the meaning and value of classroom events (Chaudron 1988).

As has been argued elsewhere (Richards 1987), it is necessary to go beyond the tabulation and quantification of classroom behaviors in order to build a theory of second language teaching. Needed are ways of discovering the higher-level concepts and thinking processes that guide the classroom teacher and ways of understanding the means by which the effective language teacher arrives at significant instructional decisions. This chapter is an attempt in this direction, and reports on a series of observations and interviews with an ESL reading teacher.

The teacher and the class

The teacher who participated in this study was completing his master's degree in teaching English as a second language at the University of Hawaii.[1] One of the classes he had taught several times was an advanced reading course for graduate students. Students in this class were either local immigrant students who had lived in Hawaii for up to five years and had attended local high schools, or foreign students who had just

1 I am grateful to Dennis Day for allowing me to scrutinize his teaching in this manner.

entered the university for graduate studies. The class met daily for sixty minutes.

The goals of this study were to use observation in order to learn more about the teaching of advanced reading and to develop a description of effective teaching. The concept of effective teaching is a familiar one in research on mainstream instruction (Berliner 1984; Blum 1984). This research deals mainly with teachers of content subjects, particularly math and reading at the elementary level. In these studies, effective teachers are defined as teachers whose students achieve higher-than-expected levels of performance on standardized achievement tests. In addition, reports of supervisors, school principals, colleagues, and students are used to identify superior teachers. In the present case, the reasons for focusing on this particular teacher's class were:

1. a highly positive impression of the teacher's teaching based on observations and comparisons with other reading teachers in the program
2. positive reports on his teaching by a supervisor
3. positive student evaluations of his teaching

The teacher agreed to be observed on a regular basis, to have some of his classes videotaped, and to be interviewed about his teaching and his class. The goal of the observations and recordings was to attempt to identify how the teacher conducted his teaching and what accounted for his apparent success. The purpose of the interviews was to find out what his teaching philosophy or approach was, what teaching strategies he employed, what learning tasks and activities he made use of, and how he used them.

The course

Although the general goals for the reading course were set out in the course description prepared by the English Language Institute, the teacher had developed a set of seven instructional objectives for his class. These were communicated to the students at the beginning of the course and referred to when appropriate throughout the semester. The objectives were:

1. to develop an awareness of reading strategies necessary for good reading comprehension
2. to expand vocabulary and to develop techniques for continued increase of vocabulary
3. to develop an awareness of linguistic and rhetorical structures found in advanced-level reading texts

4. to increase reading speed and fluency
5. to promote an interest in different types of reading materials
6. to provide individual feedback on progress in improving reading skills
7. to provide practice in extensive reading

The materials used in the class consisted of two texts – a vocabulary building text and an advanced reading text – and the SRA kit.[2]

Observation of a lesson

What follows is both a report of one of the teacher's lessons, based on analysis of the video recording, and information obtained from interviews with the teacher. The lesson discussed here occurred about halfway through the semester. During the course of the lesson, four different activities took place:

1. Students worked on the Reading for Understanding section of the SRA kit, focusing on inferencing skills.
2. Students worked with the rate-builder portion of the SRA kit, focusing on reading fluency.
3. Students worked on exercises from the vocabulary text.
4. Students began an extensive reading activity.

These activities were selected to address objectives 1, 2, 3, 4, 6, and 7.

Notes on the lesson

The lesson begins promptly. The teacher writes a brief lesson outline on the board, listing the four activities that will constitute the lesson. This is to give students (Ss) an awareness of what activities they are going to take part in, what will be expected of them during the lesson, and to give them a sense that they are taking part in activities that are planned and structured.

ACTIVITY 1: INFERENCING SKILLS

Students are instructed to form pairs and work on cards from the Reading for Understanding section of the SRA kit. The cards contain ten short passages. Beneath each passage is a set of four choices for completing the passage. For example:

2 SRA READING LABORATORY is a set of materials published by Science Research Associates, designed for students in grades 9 to 12. The kit contains multilevel individualized learning materials focusing on reading and study skills.

Physiology and chemistry are two sciences that contribute directly to our well-being. Laboratory scientists, however, cannot afford to concern themselves exclusively with the utilitarian possibilities of their research. The major theoretical advances in the sciences came from the researchers absorbed in their work as something vitally interesting in itself. They devoted themselves to the investigation of particular phenomena and relationships without bothering about

A. making practical applications.
B. investigating theoretical models.
C. studying physiology and chemistry.
D. cooperating with other scientists.

Students form pairs and discuss their choices. The teacher explains that this kind of activity is designed to be completed individually, but he regards individual use of the materials as testing rather than teaching, since Ss get no feedback on their performance if they work alone. He prefers Ss to work in pairs and to verbalize aloud their reasoning in deciding on particular answers to the comprehension questions. The Ss spend about fifteen minutes on this activity. The teacher explains that Ss should work through a progression of the cards graded according to difficulty, recording their performance on a graph. He stops using the cards when Ss reach a certain level because he finds that student performance is more variable when Ss reach a higher level, perhaps because the materials are not designed for ESL learners but are intended for use by native speakers. Topics are often too culturally specific at the more advanced levels. At this stage Ss move into reading materials taken from their regular academic courses.

As the activity progresses, the teacher moves about, checking how the Ss are doing and answering any questions they may have. Selecting the right answer to the questions requires Ss to make inferences and to deal with all of the information that has been presented in the passage, or to make use of cues within the text. In responding to questions, however, the teacher consistently refers Ss back to the text and draws their attention to cues they should be able to use to identify the meaning of a word or to select the correct answer. For example:

S: What does *torso* mean here?
T: *(pointing to a word in the passage)* It's something to do with this
   word – right?
S: With the human form?
T: Right. It's not the head and it's not the legs.
S: The part in between?
T: Yeah.

In answer to another student's query about the meaning of a word, the teacher points to another word in the text and asks:

T: What do you think it has to do with the meaning of this word?
S: Is it the opposite?
T: That's right.

After Ss have worked for about fifteen minutes on the cards, the teacher asks them to put them aside and the next activity begins.

ACTIVITY 2: READING FLUENCY

This activity involves the use of comprehension cards from the SRA kit. Ss choose a card that contains a text of perhaps two to three pages, followed by detailed comprehension questions. The goal is for Ss to try to increase their reading speed by answering the questions within a time limit. The teacher explains that he uses this activity to focus on choosing appropriate strategies for reading a text. Ss are given a choice of four different strategies for reading a text. In order to select a strategy, Ss first skim quickly through the text to get a rough idea of what it is about and how difficult it is. Based on this initial reading they then choose a suitable strategy. The four strategies are:

Strategy A: Read the text, read the comprehension questions, then go back and skim for answers. This is the most detailed way of reading the text.
Strategy B: Read the questions, read the text carefully to find the answers, then go back and check the answers against the questions.
Strategy C: Skim the text, read the questions, then scan for the answers.
Strategy D: Read the questions, then skim for the answers. This is the fastest strategy.

The teacher begins by writing the choices on the board:

A	B	C	D
Read	Questions	Skim	Questions
Questions	Read	Questions	Skim
Skim		Scan	

The Ss go to the reading kit and select a card to work with. The teacher asks a few Ss around the class about the text they have chosen.

T: What passage are you going to read?
S1: Malaria.
T: Do you know much about that topic?
S1: Not really.
T: So what strategy are you going to choose?
S1: Strategy B.
T: So you want to read it a little more slowly.
S1: Yes.

T: *(to another student)* What's your topic?
S2: Methods of experiments in science.
T: How do you feel about that?
S2: I'll choose A.

The teacher explains that he checks to see what strategy the student has chosen and why he or she has chosen it. Generally Ss will choose a slower strategy if they are unfamiliar with the topic. The teacher is trying to sensitize the Ss to the fact that they should choose strategies appropriate to the kinds of material they are reading. Ss spend about three minutes on each card and are under pressure to choose a strategy that will enable them to read the card quickly. They record their scores throughout the semester and work on the cards once or twice a week. The teacher finds a general improvement in their reading speed and comprehension levels throughout the semester. Once the Ss have each completed a card, the teacher checks their scores and their timing and asks which strategy they used. If their score is not very good, he asks if they think a different strategy would have been better.

T: What did you get, Maria?
S1: I got a 5. I think I misread this sentence right here.
T: How did you read it? What strategy did you use?
S1: C.
T: So you read it pretty fast. *(to another student)* How did you do?
S2: Not so good.
T: You chose B for this passage. Do you think if you had read it more slowly it would have helped?
S2: Yes. The subject is not clear, not too easy for me. The topic is about stamps.

After about ten minutes the next activity begins.

ACTIVITY 3: VOCABULARY

The teacher then announces the next activity and the amount of time Ss should spend on it (about ten minutes). The teacher explains that he sets a time limit for each phase of the lesson to make sure that Ss work seriously on each activity and attempt to get through it within the allotted time. The third activity involves working with the vocabulary-building text. As Ss return their SRA cards to the kit (which takes a little time), the teacher uses this time to read out the students' answers to a homework assignment from the text. The students have written sentences using new words they have studied, and the teacher reads sentences aloud and asks the class to comment on them. The teacher regards this activity as a time filler to occupy the students while they are getting their cards back into the SRA kit. Ss then begin work on exercises from the vocabulary text.

The exercises in the book deal with vocabulary in context, analogies, derivations, collocations, definitions, and paraphrases. One set of exercises requires students to decide if the second sentence in a pair is true or false based on how the word is used in a preceding sentence. For example,

Unions often *agitate* employers by striking to get better working conditions for union members.

It would be reasonable to expect some emotional response from a friend you have *agitated*. True False

As with the first activity in the lesson, even though the exercises could be completed individually, the teacher asks the Ss to work in pairs and to negotiate and discuss their answers. Then he checks their answers by having a student read his or her answer aloud. Rather than confirm whether the answer is correct, the teacher asks the other Ss to give their opinion.

ACTIVITY 4: AN EXTENSIVE READING ACTIVITY

The last activity of the lesson involves reading a lengthy article from one of the class texts. The teacher explains that this is a study-skills exercise dealing with how to approach a text that is going to be read intensively, such as a chapter in a textbook or an article. The teacher explains that he uses a modification of the SQ4R technique (Survey, Question, Read, Recite, Review, Reflect),[3] but has added a K for "Knowledge of the World" to the beginning of the acronym. This means that before Ss begin reading the passage, they will take part in a prereading activity designed to activate background knowledge about the topic.

The article they are going to read is on the Cultural Revolution in

---

3 The SQ4R technique involves the following steps. *Survey:* Ss look through the chapter to find out how long it is; what charts, pictures, questions, headings, summaries, etc., it contains; and think about what can be learned from the chapter, how useful the information might be, how it relates to their class, etc.

Question: Each heading and subheading is turned into a question.

Read: The student reads purposefully to answer the questions, keeping purpose in mind. Students mark main ideas and write question marks beside any sentence that they do not understand.

Recite: After reading a paragraph, the student covers it and checks it to see if the main idea can be understood or expressed in the student's own words. If not, it is marked with a question mark to indicate that rereading is necessary.

Review: After finishing, the student looks back at the markings and reviews the main ideas noted. Any sections not understood are reread.

Reflect: After reading the chapter, the student reflects on how useful the information will be. The student pays attention to the connections between the chapter and the student's own knowledge so that it can be remembered when needed.

China. Before they begin reading, the teacher asks each student to write down three facts about how China has changed in the last twenty years. He then collects the comments and invites three students from China to move to the front of the class, read the students' comments to the class, and comment briefly on them. Following this, the teacher reminds the Ss of the SQ4R technique and the Ss begin reading the chapter individually. The remainder of the lesson is taken up with this activity, and discussion of the comprehension questions is assigned to the next class. After some eight minutes the teacher announces that time is up and the class concludes.

Reflections on the lesson

The purpose of observing this teacher's class was to attempt to identify what went on in his class and why. Although description of what happens in a lesson is relatively easy, moving beyond description to interpretation and evaluation is more difficult. The observer tries to avoid being anecdotal and subjective, merely describing his or her own value system. However, this risk has to be taken in order to try to understand the meaning and value of real classroom events.

Having viewed the video of the lesson described here many times and explored with the teacher his philosophy of teaching, I was able to formulate the following principles to account for why this particular lesson took the form it did, why this lesson can be described as an effective one, and how this teacher approaches the teaching of reading.

1. Instructional objectives are used to guide and organize lessons. The teacher uses statements of course objectives to help him plan and organize his teaching. For the lesson observed, the teacher was able to formulate what the lesson was intended to accomplish and how its goals were to be achieved. Although the objectives he used were not stated as *behavioral* objectives, they nonetheless served as a way of clarifying and formulating his own intentions and selecting appropriate learning experiences.

2. The teacher has a comprehensive theory of the nature of reading in a second language, and refers to this in planning his teaching. The teacher does not rely on "common sense" or a quest for lively and interesting techniques to occupy class time. Rather, he refers to his understanding of the nature of the second language reading process, to his understanding of second language reading strategies, and to schema theory and the role of background knowledge in reading, and uses this information to help him select and plan learning experiences. The lesson observed demonstrated the truth of the saying that "there is nothing so practical as a good theory."

3. *Class time is used for learning.* In this lesson, as in other lessons observed, the teacher consciously attempted to maximize the amount of class time spent on learning. Students were on-task for some fifty out of the sixty minutes of class time, the remaining time being taken up with procedural matters. Even time needed for classroom logistics (such as when students returned their SRA cards to the kit) was utilized productively as an opportunity to check students' answers to a homework assignment.

4. *Instructional activities have a teaching rather than a testing focus.* On a number of occasions, the teacher justified his departure from the format suggested in the materials or class text by distinguishing between a teaching versus a testing focus in activities. Activities with a teaching focus provide opportunities for learners to develop or improve their use and understanding of reading skills and strategies. Activities with a testing focus require learners to demonstrate how well they can use strategies and skills. The teacher emphasized that more opportunities are provided for learning through pair work rather than individual work, for example, and by having students verbally express the decision-making processes they employed in arriving at the answer to a question or the meaning of a word. The teacher commented, "The only way I believe the students can tap into the reading process itself is by talking about it, by talking about what they do as they read, to verbalize what they are doing when they are reading."

5. *Lessons have a clear structure.* In the lessons observed, the teacher communicated to the students at the beginning of the lesson the kinds of activities they would be doing and the order in which they would do them. Purposes for activities were clear. When students moved into a new task, the teacher announced the time allowed for completing the activity, to give the students a time frame and endpoint for the activity.

6. *A variety of different activities are used during each lesson.* The teacher provides a variety of different learning experiences within lessons. In the lesson observed, four different activities were used, and this variation in activities may have contributed to the positive attitude of the students toward the classroom tasks as well as the active pacing of the lesson.

7. *Classroom activities give students opportunities to get feedback on their reading performance.* In this lesson, students were not merely practicing reading. They were also getting information about the kind of

reading strategies they were using for different reading tasks and how effective those strategies were – a primary goal of all reading lessons, according to the teacher.

8. Instructional activities relate to real-world reading purposes. In the lesson there was a progression from "micro" activities, which dealt with specific reading strategies and were based on specially prepared peda-gogical materials, to a "macro" activity, which required students to integrate the different strategies in reading a longer academic article. The teacher explained that as soon as is appropriate, students bring their own textbooks to class and these are used as the basis for many classroom activities.

9. Instruction is learner focused. Although several opportunities arose during the lesson for the teacher to lecture or talk about reading strat-egies, he consciously stepped back and encouraged the learners to try to work things out by themselves. The teacher sees his role as that of a consultant or resource person in this class.

These principles appear to explain why the teacher approaches the teach-ing of reading in the way he does, and why the lesson that was observed took the form it did. They go a considerable way toward explaining why the lesson was an effective one and why the teacher can be described as an effective teacher of reading. Of course, in order to validate the principles suggested here, it would be necessary to observe the teacher and the class over a much longer period of time. But how useful is this approach to the understanding of teaching?

Conclusions

The approach to the study of teaching illustrated here is a *qualitative* one. Qualitative research focuses on higher-level generalizations about the phenomenon being studied and makes use of introspective and ob-servational approaches to gathering data. It seeks to understand the meaning and value of the phenomenon being examined. A quantitative approach, on the other hand, focuses on isolating and measuring in precise quantifiable terms causes and effects, treatments, and outcomes. Quantitative research has a degree of scientific rigor often said to be lacking in qualitative research. As Van Lier (1988: xiv) observes, quan-titative research leads to

finding cause-effect relationships between certain actions and their outcomes. This aim leads to a concern with strong correlations, levels of significance, definability and control of variables, and all the other requirements of scientific method. The price that is paid for scientific control is an inevitable neglect of the social context of the interaction between teachers and learners. Without this social context it is difficult to see how classroom interaction can be understood and what cause-effect relationships, if they can ever be conclusively established, really mean. At the risk of oversimplification, research can be divided into a type which wants to obtain *proof* and a type which wants to *understand*.

Both kinds of research are needed, and their usefulness depends on what the researcher wants to find out. A qualitative approach is appropriate here because the principles of effective teaching that have been examined in this chapter cannot all be conveyed in operational terms but are crucially dependent upon the teacher's understanding of the nature of reading, philosophy of teaching, and theory of second language teaching and learning. Identifying this kind of information requires a qualitative rather than a quantitative approach to the study of teaching. While the information arrived at through this process does not have the kind of reliability obtained from controlled experimental studies or from multiple independent coding of the same events, it is still invaluable in helping us understand the nature of teaching and learning and the kinds of planning and decision making that teachers use.

At the same time, it should be stressed that the process of investigating teaching is valuable for its own sake (see Chapter 7). Teachers and teachers-in-preparation need to be involved in the investigation of their own teaching and the teaching of others in order to generate an understanding of how good teaching comes about. It is this process of looking at teaching and reflecting about it that is of greatest value, rather than the results of a particular investigation. In teacher education, this involves novice teachers working with experienced teachers, observing them at work, and gradually exploring with them the hidden dimensions of their classrooms. For the reflective teacher, it involves self-monitoring and self-investigation – an ongoing program of gathering data about one's own teaching through journal accounts, self-reports, or audio or video recordings, in order to gain a deeper understanding of one's own teaching.

Discussion topics and activities

1. Examine the criteria for determining whether the teacher described in this chapter was effective (p. 89). What other criteria could be used to select an effective teacher?
2. Prepare a set of questions that you could use to interview a reading teacher, in order to understand his or her philosophy of teaching

and what the teacher considers effective teaching of reading to be. Then interview a reading teacher using your questions. Compare your findings with those of other students.

3. Examine the teacher's objectives for his class on pages 89–90. Would you use the same objectives if teaching an advanced reading class of this kind?

4. Discuss the difference between "teaching" and "testing." Select an activity that could be used in a reading class, and discuss how it could be presented (a) to have primarily a teaching focus and (b) to have primarily a testing focus. How was the activity presented differently in each case?

5. Review the principles that the teacher seems to be following (pp. 95–97) and examine each principle in turn. How important are these principles to you? Draw up a list of your own principles for teaching a reading class, and then compare them with other students.

6. "There is nothing so practical as a good theory." Do you agree? Can you have good practice without theory? What is the relation of theory to practice?

7. If possible, make arrangements to observe an experienced reading teacher's class. Before you do your observation, interview the teacher using the questions you prepared in question 2. Then observe the teacher's class. How effective was it? Draw up a list of the principles the teacher seemed to follow.

8. Prepare a lesson plan for a reading class that reflects the principles you prepared in question 5. Then compare your lesson plans with plans prepared by other students. How do they differ?

6 From meaning into words: writing in a second or foreign language

Learning to write in either a first or second language is one of the most difficult tasks a learner encounters and one that few people can be said to fully master. Many native speakers leave school with a poor command of writing. Even at university level, students require further instruction in writing, providing employment for the teams of instructors in college English departments who teach courses in freshman composition. Learning to write well is a difficult and lengthy process, one that induces anxiety and frustration in many learners.

Yet good writing skills are essential to academic success and a requirement for many occupations and professions. In adult life, people's writing needs are both institutional and personal (Davies and Widdowson 1974). Institutional writing is writing produced in a professional or institutional role, such as that of businessperson, teacher, or student, and conforms to institutional conventions. Personal writing includes personal letters and creative writing. In an ESL writing program, purposes are much more restricted. Most school-related writing is destined either for the teacher (e.g., essays, assignments) or for the learners themselves (e.g., notes, summaries). Writing is used either as evidence of successful learning or as a means of learning. Because writing leads to a product that can be examined and reviewed immediately, it provides feedback to the teacher and learner on what has been understood. It can also guide the process of understanding and organizing ideas during reading or listening (Emig 1971). Writing will therefore continue to occupy a prominent role in the curriculum. But why should the teaching and learning of writing be so problematic? How can writing be addressed in the second language curriculum? In this chapter, these questions will be addressed by first examining the nature of written discourse and then by considering approaches to the teaching of writing in a second language.

Differences between written and spoken discourse

Part of the difficulty of learning to write well is due to the difference between spoken and written discourse. Whereas the rules of spoken discourse are acquired through conversation and do not require instruc-

100

tion, the rules of written discourse are largely learned through instruction and practice. The fact that written discourse reflects very different rules from spoken language may account for the difficulties learners have in mastering the ability to write well. Olson (1977) suggests that as a writing system evolves for a language (or, by extension, as a learner develops proficiency in writing), a linguistic system develops that must be able to express explicit autonomous statements. Writing is not "merely a way of recording language by means of visible marks," as the American linguist Leonard Bloomfield once remarked. Whereas spoken language is primarily listener oriented and is used to promote social interaction (see Chapter 8), written language is primarily transactional or message oriented (Brown and Yule 1983). The goal of written language is to convey information accurately, effectively, and appropriately; and to do this written language has to be more explicit than spoken discourse.

Written language needs to be explicit because the audience for a written text may be unknown to the writer, particularly with writing intended for publication. Consequently the amount of shared knowledge between writer and reader is much less than that usually found between speaker and listener. In conversation, the participants often share background knowledge about a topic, and so a great deal can be left unsaid or merely implied. In writing, however, no such assumptions can usually be made. Writing is "decontextualized" and must provide its own context, expressing meanings explicitly. Written language hence employs a different syntax and vocabulary from spoken discourse. It also has a more elaborated linguistic system characterized by the use of complex rather than simple clauses, a greater variety of clause types, more specific vocabulary, a higher frequency of complex verb phrases and tenses, and a greater variety of devices for expressing such syntactic processes as relativization, nominalization, and complementization (Brown and Yule 1983). It is in this sense that Olson speaks of written language as an autonomous system.

Producing written discourse

It is not merely the linguistic organization of written discourse that makes writing a difficult skill to acquire. The process of moving from concepts, thoughts, and ideas to written text is complex. A written text represents the product of a series of complicated mental operations (Clark and Clark 1977: 226–58). After having decided on a meaning to be expressed, the writer has to consider the genre of text he or she is trying to write (e.g., a story, a description, an explanation), the type of style he or she is trying to create (e.g., neutral, expressive, casual), the purpose to be achieved (e.g., to persuade, to inform, to warn), and the amount of detail that is needed in order to achieve the writer's purpose. Clark and Clark (1977: 232–3) illustrate the kinds of decisions writers must face in writing descriptions. In describing a landscape, for example, a series of problems present themselves:

1. *Level.* At what level should it be described? Should the writer merely say, "I saw a beautiful landscape?", or should every last leaf and pebble be mentioned?
2. *Content.* Given the level, which parts should be included and which should be omitted? Normally, the landscape will be too complicated to include everything, so the writer must pick and choose.
3. *Order.* Given the parts the writer has decided to include, what order should they be put in? Should they be described from left to right, from nearest to farthest, from most to least important, from largest to smallest, or how?
4. *Relations.* For the given level, content, and order, how should the parts be related to each other? Is it enough for the parts to be listed as present, or should each be given a precise location with respect to the rest?

The writer's solution to these problems hangs ultimately on his or her purpose. Does the writer want the reader to be able to recreate the objective details of the scene? Does the writer want to highlight one object and describe its relation to everything else? Or does he or she want to evoke a diffuse mood?

Readability and reader-based prose

What the writer ultimately writes as a product of complex cognitive and linguistic planning and decision making is not necessarily "good" writing – it must also be easy to read. Good writing acknowledges the reader. Flower (1979; and Flower and Hayes 1980, 1981) suggests that in composing a text, writers usually begin with a view of themselves as readers, and gradually introduce the reader's perspective during the process of revision. There is a gradual movement from writer-based to reader-based prose throughout the composing process. This reflects the fact that good writers aim to make their writing unambiguous for the reader. Although readers have more time available to process written discourse than listeners do in processing spoken discourse, there are limitations on what readers can comfortably process. Herbert Spencer (cited in Hirsch 1977: 78) expressed this eloquently more than one hundred years ago:

A reader or listener has at each moment but a limited amount of mental power available. To recognize and interpret the symbols presented to him requires part of this power; to arrange and combine the images suggested by them requires a further part; and only that part which remains can be used for framing the thought expressed. Hence the more time and attention it takes to receive and understand each sentence, the less time and attention can be given to the contained idea; and the less vividly will that idea be conceived.

The readability of a text depends on the ease with which the reader can identify and integrate its underlying propositions. If the reader's short-term memory is overloaded with information that can be related to two or more possible interpretations, the reader may have to stop and read again. Hirsch (1977), in an illuminating discussion of readability and prose style, observed that English prose has gradually become more readable over the centuries, as writers opted for simpler sentence structure in which possibilities for ambiguous assignment of constituents were reduced. He compares the same passage from a sixteenth-century English translation of Boccaccio's *Decameron* with an eighteenth-century translation. The sixteenth-century version reads like this:

Saladin, whose valiance was so great that not only the same from base estate advanced him to be Sultan of Babylon, but also thereby he won diverse victories over the Saracen kings and Christians; who through his manifold wars and magnificent triumphs, having expended all his treasure, and for the execution of one exploit lacking a great sum of money, knew not where to have the same so readily as he had occasion to employ it. At length he called to remembrance a rich Jew named Melchizedech, that lent out money for interest in Alexandria. (Hirsch 1977: 61)

The eighteenth-century translation is more readable, because the syntax and sentence structure help the reader identify propositions in the text more readily, and there are fewer possibilities of multiple interpretations.

Saladin was so brave and great a man, that he had raised himself from an inconsiderable person to be Sultan of Babylon, and also gave him many signal victories over both the Saracen and Christian princes. This monarch having in diverse wars and by many extraordinary expenses, run through all his treasure, some urgent occasion fell out that he wanted a large sum of money. Not knowing which way he might raise enough to answer his necessities, he at last called to mind a rich Jew of Alexandria named Melchizedech, who lent out money on interest. (Hirsch 1977: 61)

Coherence and cohesion

While readability in the sense discussed in the previous section is primarily a factor at the level of individual sentences in a text, patterns of organization and structure also exist at higher levels of organization.

103

The notion of "coherence" is used to refer to the overall semantic structure and unity of a text. Coherence is a fundamental requirement of written discourse. Although it is a fuzzy concept that is difficult to define, coherence is an essential practical construct in discussing the quality of written discourse. According to Canale (1982: 5–6), for a text to have coherence the following conditions must be met:

1. Development: Presentation of ideas must be orderly and convey a sense of direction.
2. Continuity: There must be consistency of facts, opinions, and writer perspective, as well as reference to previously mentioned ideas. Newly introduced ideas must be relevant.
3. Balance: A relative emphasis (main or supportive) must be accorded each idea.
4. Completeness: The ideas presented must provide a sufficiently thorough discourse.

A component of coherence is the text structure, or schema, the text reflects. Different types of writing (e.g., narratives, instructions, reports, business letters) reflect specific kinds of text structures, and will be judged as more or less appropriate and coherent according to the degree of fit between the genre and the text structure expected for that genre. For example, a common text structure, or schema, according to Hoey (1979, 1983) is the *problem-solution* structure, found in many scientific papers. This has been represented as having the following organization:

1. Introduction
   (a) Direct the reader's attention to the subject or problem.
   (b) Explain your experience with the subject – the reasons why you can write with authority.
   (c) Establish bridges with the readers by pointing out shared beliefs, attitudes, and experiences.
2. Background
   (a) Explain the nature of the problem, its history, and causes.
   (b) Explain its relevance to the reader's problems, desires, and interests – the reasons why the problem is important to the reader.
3. Argument
   (a) State the major premise. Include any information necessary to make it clear and acceptable.
   (b) State the minor premise, again including necessary information.
   (c) State your conclusion.

    (d) Show your position is better by pointing out defects in the premise or inferences of alternative positions. Explain why the alternatives cannot solve the problem; or if they can, why your solution solves it better.

4. Conclusion

    (a) Explain the implications of your argument.

    (b) Summarize your argument: the problem (2a), your conclusion (3c), and the reasons for accepting it (3a and 3b).

A coherent and appropriately written scientific paper should reflect this kind of text structure. Every type of writing reflects a particular kind of text or discourse structure, and the good writer is able to draw on these discourse patterns in organizing his or her writing. Paragraphs too have their own structures:

Some paragraphs proceed from the general to the specific, or from the particular to the general; others alternate topics in order to compare and contrast; and still others lay out details in a chronological order, a spatial order, or an order that builds to a climax. People "know" that paragraphs have structure, for they object to ones that do not conform to these possibilities. (Clark and Clark 1977: 168)

A complementary perspective on the unity of text is that of *cohesion*. Whereas coherence refers to the way in which the ideas in a text give it a sense of semantic unity, cohesion refers to the linking relationships that are explicitly expressed in the surface structure of the text (Halliday and Hasan 1976). For Halliday and Hasan, cohesion is achieved through the use of a variety of lexical and grammatical relationships between items within sentences in the text. They identify five types of cohesive ties: reference, substitution, ellipsis, conjunction, and lexical:

1. *Reference:* The children did not come because *they* wanted to stay inside.
2. *Substitution:* We wanted to buy some glasses and finally bought some French *ones*.
3. *Ellipsis:* "Would you like to hear another verse? I know twelve (verses) more."
4. *Conjunction:* "I was not informed. *Otherwise* I would have taken some action."
5. *Lexical:* Henry presented her with his own *portrait*. As it happened, she had always wanted a *portrait* of Henry.

Appropriate uses of cohesive devices support the overall coherence of writing and represent another dimension of writing that a writer has to master.

    There are therefore many dimensions to written discourse, both at the macro level of text structure and at the micro level of syntax and vocabulary. A number of different dimensions of planning and decision making are involved in producing writing that reflects the norms and conventions of written discourse. Let us now consider how these dimensions have been addressed in second and foreign language writing curriculums.

The product-focused approach

The nature and significance of writing have traditionally been under-estimated in language teaching. In second and foreign language programs, the teaching of second language writing has often been synonymous with the teaching of grammar or sentence structure. This view of writing reflects the principles of audiolingual theory, from which it is derived, as well as the opinion of earlier generations of linguists, who saw writing as the written form of spoken language. Speech was considered primary in the Audiolingual Approach, and writing "served to reinforce speech in that it stressed mastery of grammatical and syntactic forms" (Raimes 1983: 6); it thus served as the basis for aural fluency.

At more advanced levels, this approach to the teaching of writing leads to practice in the structure and organization of different kinds of paragraphs and texts. Because the focus is essentially on the ability to produce correct texts or "products," this approach to teaching writing is referred to as the *product approach*. The main assumptions and features of the product approach in second language teaching are:

1. Learners have specific writing needs, either for institutional writing or personal writing.
2. The goal of a writing program is to teach students to be able to produce the kinds of written texts they will most frequently encounter in educational, institutional, and/or personal contexts. The writing program will focus on the patterns and forms of organization used in different kinds of written texts (e.g., differences between descriptive, narrative, expository, and persuasive writing; formats used to present information in an essay or report; different ways of organizing information in paragraphs).
3. The rhetorical patterns and grammatical rules used in different kinds of texts are presented in model compositions, which are constructed to display the rules that learners should use in their own writing.
4. Correct sentence structure is an essential component of writing; grammatical skills receive considerable emphasis.
5. Errors in writing are avoided by providing learners with models to

follow or by guiding and controlling what learners write to prevent them from making errors.

6. The mechanics of writing are also taught: handwriting, capitalization, punctuation, and spelling.

Thus the primary emphasis is on providing practice in producing different kinds of texts. A secondary goal is to prevent students from producing errors. As Bright and McGregor express it:

The pupil does not learn from his mistakes. If he did, the more mistakes he made, the more he would learn. Common experience, however, proves that the pupil who makes the most mistakes is the one who has learnt and will learn least. In theory no mistake should ever appear in writing, though it must be admitted that this ideal is unattainable in practice. (1970: 130)

Hence, instead of allowing students freedom to create their own compositions, techniques of "controlled composition" or "guided writing" are used, for they do not require the student to do any actual composition. Techniques used in a product approach often begin with controlled writing exercises and gradually move toward freer writing once the learner has memorized the structures to be followed. Techniques include:

– providing models to which learners make minor changes and substitutions
– expanding an outline or summary
– constructing paragraphs from frames, tables, and other guides
– producing a text through answering a set of questions
– sentence combining: developing complex sentences following different rules of combination

This approach is sometimes known as a "prose model approach" when used for teaching composition skills to native speakers. According to Eschholz (1980: 22) this is based on the strategy of Read, Analyze, and Write:

A typical unit in a prose model writing class might proceed as follows. In preparation for writing an essay of comparison-contrast, students are asked to read Bruce Catton's "Grant and Lee: A Study in Contrasts," a classic example of this particular rhetorical mode. Next, students are asked to study the essay, answering questions about Catton's thesis, organization, paragraph development, sentence structure, diction, and so on. In class, the teacher focuses attention on the writer's purpose and his overall organization, perhaps analyzing several sample passages to illustrate Catton's "block-by-block" organizational plan or his effective use of transitions. Finally, each student is asked to write his or her own comparison-contrast essay, using Catton's essay as the model.

The overall emphasis in the product approach, as it is used both with first and second/foreign language learners, is hence on the form of the finished product that the student produces rather than on the process of writing. From this perspective, as a learner's writing proficiency increases, the learner develops the capacity to handle more complex writing tasks. As this happens, the learner uses a greater variety of rhetorical and discourse modes and masters more subtle and complex aspects of paragraph and sentence organization.

The process approach

In recent years, writing researchers have pointed out the limitations of a product approach to the teaching of writing. A product approach concentrates on ends rather than means. By focusing on the form and structure of writing rather than on how writers create writing that has form and structure, the composing processes of good writers are ignored. But as Murray observes, "Process cannot be inferred from product any more than a pig can be inferred from a sausage" (1980: 3). If our goal in teaching writing is to develop fluent writers, it is necessary to examine how fluent writers compose and to reexamine our writing methodology in the light of this information.

Cognitive processes in writing

The focus of recent research on writing has been on the different kinds of strategies and cognitive activities that a writer engages in when writing. These can be investigated by using such procedures as (a) observing writers as they write; (b) interviewing writers before and after writing to determine how they dealt with particular aspects of a writing task; (c) having writers verbalize some of the decisions they are making as they write; (d) examining writers' journal accounts of their writing processes; (e) making ethnographic studies of writing classes. Raimes (1985: 229) reports that from this research, a composite picture is emerging of what experienced writers do:

They consider purpose and audience. They consult their own background knowledge. They let ideas incubate. They plan. As they write, they read back over what they have written... Contrary to what many textbooks advise, writers do not follow a neat sequence of planning, organizing, writing, and then revising. For while a writer's product – the finished essay, story, or novel – is presented in lines, the process that produces it is not linear at all.

Murray (1980) distinguishes three stages in writing: rehearsing, drafting, and revising. *Rehearsing*, or *prewriting*, involves finding a topic; finding ideas about the topic; thinking about the topic; letting ideas interact, develop, and organize themselves; and thinking about the audience and the purpose of the writing task. At this stage the writer may not know how many of the ideas or how much of the information will be used. *Drafting* involves getting ideas onto paper in rough form. The writer sketches out an idea, examines it, and follows it through for a while – perhaps letting it follow its own course. What has been written serves to generate further ideas, plans, and goals. Thus the process of writing creates its own meaning. The writer may also go back to the rehearsing phase, and alternate between the rehearsing and drafting phases. *Revising* involves evaluating what has been written and making deletions or additions as necessary, "to help the writing say what it intends to say" (Murray 1980: 5). However, as Raimes points out, revising can occur at any time in the composing process.

Research on writing strategies is important for the insights it yields into differences between skilled and unskilled writers. As we saw in Chapter 2, an unskilled writer is not simply one who cannot produce a good writing product. It is one who uses inappropriate writing behaviors and processes when writing. The Appendix presents a summary of the differences between strategies employed by skilled and unskilled writers.

Research into the processes of composition also raises important implications for the methodology of teaching writing in a second or foreign language. First, it appears that an undue concern with the formal aspects of writing can impede the development of efficient writing strategies. In addition, successful writers appear to produce better-quality writing because they use more appropriate writing processes. Their successful use of rehearsing, drafting, and revising behaviors ultimately gives them better control both of the content and form of what they write. A number of fundamental changes toward the teaching of writing are hence emerging from attempts to incorporate a process perspective into second language writing programs. These changes affect the roles of learners, the roles of teachers, and the kinds of instructional activities that are employed in the writing classroom.

THE ROLE OF LEARNERS

Case studies of successful second and foreign language writing programs (see Zamel 1987) reveal that in process-focused classrooms there is a shift from language-focused activities to learner-centered tasks in which students assume greater control over what they write, how they write it, and the evaluation of their own writing. In a program described by Diaz, Moll, and Mehan (cited in Zamel 1987: 704–5),

students became engaged in their own ethnographic research, collecting data from their own community, and produced writing based on their analysis of this information. Their skills, experiences and strengths became the basis for further instruction, and responsibility for and control of learning shifted from teacher to student. In this way students who would otherwise do little or no classroom writing because of their language difficulties were better prepared for academic work in English.

Learners now have more opportunities for meaningful writing, are less dependent on the teacher, and work collaboratively with other students. Different patterns of classroom interaction may thus develop, as is seen in Carey (1986). She describes a writing workshop for elementary-school children where the challenge was "presenting the writing process as exploratory, provisional, and recursive, without directly explaining that it was so. The children's challenge was to find purpose, audience and content for their composing" (p. 52). Carey (p. 53) describes how throughout the workshop, children selected topics to write about, initiated collaborative writing, and developed characteristic interaction patterns with other learners:

1. *Topics* came from experience at home and in school and from imitation of peers. "Cult" figures like Garfield and literary forms like choose-your-own-adventure books provided models.
2. *Writing together evolved from social talk* and created a context for the composing process that offered multiple points of view, natural motivation, and minimized the need for direct teaching.
3. *Two patterns of collaboration developed:* expert/novice, novice/novice. Students used their strengths to help others or worked through composing problems together, alternating combat and negotiation. Collaboration took students through the writing process, without isolating stages or strategies.
4. *The teacher role* became that of adult writer with useful experience to be shared on request as part of collaboration. The children's composing rhythms dictated the appropriate moment. In addition a close relationship akin to reading-together with young children developed between adult and child.
5. While the preferred mode was narrative, *collaborators used techniques of explanation and persuasion* to select appropriate materials and story lines, or to resolve disputes.
6. *Drawing was used extensively to find, explore, and revise ideas.*
7. *Revision* meant reworking a familiar topic rather than redrafting the same piece. An essential part of revision was permission to abandon a piece or leave it unfinished without a sense of failure.
8. Within the limits of the workshop, *participants gained confidence, explored the writing process and their own resources, and in at least one case improved mechanical proficiency.*

THE ROLE OF THE TEACHER

The teacher's role is likewise redefined and renegotiated in a process-focused classroom. Rather than attempting to constrain learners to ensure that they produce correct writing, teachers act as facilitators, organizing writing experiences that enable the learner to develop effective composing strategies. The teacher is also an investigator of the writing processes employed by the students, using observation and discussion to identify successful approaches to different aspects of the writing process. Hughey et al. (1983: 48) present a comprehensive list of roles for teachers in a writing program.

They keep the writing task clear, simple, and straightforward.
They teach the writing process.
They analyze and diagnose a writing product.
They establish short-term and long-term goals for each student.
They balance classroom activities, providing some for individuals and some for groups.
They develop meaningful assignments.
They provide a real audience: an audience other than the teacher.
They make student papers available to students: they allow students to see their own body of work develop.
They move from the known to the unknown and utilize the student's previous knowledge.
They provide writing activities which reinforce reading, listening, and speaking skills.
They provide heuristics for invention, purpose, and audience.
They outline clearly the goals for each writing assignment.
They teach the conventions of spelling, punctuation, and capitalization.
They teach the principles – rules, conventions, and guidelines of writing – as a means to develop thoughts, order ideas, and communicate these ideas in a significant way.

Observation of teachers in action in the writing classroom, however, is needed to confirm these suggestions. With an advanced writing class, Carey (1986: 64) reports that the roles of learners and teacher were different from the elementary class she described earlier:

The role of expert initially fell to the instructor because students lacked confidence, but also because the writing tasks they had to master were not the familiar narrative model we internalise from earliest reading and talking about events. The students had to grapple with challenging ideas as well as the demandingly precise style of expository and argumentative writing. It was natural that they should turn to an expert for help. But as the course developed and the undergraduates shared the design of each session my role subtly shifted.

I wrote the same assignments to demonstrate composing and test the viability of the topics in front of the students, sharing the composing problems and successes that each student was experiencing. And since the students helped revise my drafts I moved closer to fellow writer and away from judge and critic. Although my writing was more polished from experience and

111

practice, the novice writers saw that the expert has failures and problems to overcome.

Different patterns of teacher–student interaction are also cited in a study by Kantor (1984). In an ethnographic study of teacher–student interaction in a high school writing class, Kantor found that the teacher's nondirective and encouraging attitude, together with the supportive and relaxed atmosphere of the classroom, enabled the class to function as a community of writers, a community that included the teacher. This brought about a relationship of trust, which encouraged students to take more risks with their writing and to be more confident about what they wrote.

KINDS OF INSTRUCTIONAL ACTIVITIES

A different approach to the design of instructional activities is needed for a process-focused approach to the teaching of writing. Activities currently used reflect a focus on the different stages in the writing process. Among those proposed by recent writing methodologists (Koch and Brazil 1978; Lindemann 1982; Proett and Gill 1986) are the following.

1. *Activities related to the rehearsing phase.* These are designed to help learners develop ideas for writing, to help generate plans for writing, to serve as an initial stimulus for writing, and to provide motivation. Examples are:

Journals. Students explore ideas and record thoughts in a journal.

Brainstorming. Students rapidly exchange information about a topic or about something they have selected to read.

Free association. Put the topic on the board. Students quickly say whatever words come to mind when they see the topic word.

Values clarification. Students compare attitudes toward a variety of specific problems and situations.

Clustering or word mapping. The writer writes a topic in the middle of a page and organizes related words and concepts in clusters around the central concept.

Ranking activities. Students rank a set of features according to priorities.

Quickwriting. Students write as much as they can in a given time (e.g., 5 minutes) on a topic, without worrying about the form of what they write.

Information-gathering activities. Students are given assignments related to a theme or topic and resources where related information can be found. These may include interviews, opinion surveys, field trips, and experiments or demonstrations.

Activities of this type may lead in to a summarizing session that prepares the students for the next phase in the writing process, in which they review their ideas and begin to focus on what they can use as a basis for writing.

2. *Activities related to the drafting/writing phase.* In this phase of the writing process, the writer moves from initial attempts to sketch out different sections of a composition toward an overall draft of the paragraph or essay. Audience, purpose, and form are now considered. The writer draws on some of the ideas generated in the rehearsing phase but develops and elaborates them as the writing process takes over. Activities may include:

Strategic questioning. Students examine a set of questions to help them focus, prioritize, and select ideas for writing. For example:
 – What do you really want to write about?
 – What is your goal?
 – What is your attitude toward this task? Why?
 – What have you learned about your topic?
 – What do you still need to find out?
 – What interests or surprises you about the topic?
 – What ideas seem to fit together?
 – What is the most important thing to know about the topic?
 – Who might want to read what you are going to write?
 (Lapp 1984)
Timed-focused writing. Students write quickly within a specified time period on a topic they have selected during prewriting.
Elaboration exercise. Students are given a sentence and collectively elaborate and develop it.
Reduction exercise. Students are given a wordy and complex paragraph and break it down into simpler sentences.
Jumbled paragraph. Students are given a jumbled paragraph and reorder the sentences.
Jumbled essay. Students are given a jumbled set of paragraphs and reorder them to make an essay.
Writing thesis statements and topic sentences. Students are given a statement from which to develop a thesis statement and a topic sentence.
Quickwriting. Students quickwrite various sections of their composition: beginnings, central sections, conclusions.
Group drafting. Students work jointly on drafting different sections of a composition.

3. *Activities related to the revising phase.* These are the editing and proofreading phases of writing. Techniques include:

Peer feedback. Students work in groups and read, criticize, and proofread their own writing.
Group-correction activities. Students are given essays containing certain

113

focused deletions (e.g., topic sentences, thesis statements, cohesive markers) and must supply the missing elements.

Rewriting exercises. Awkward sentences or confusing paragraphs from student essays are distributed and rewritten by students.

Revising heuristics. Students examine a set of questions that prepare them for revision activities. For example:

- In composing your draft, what was the biggest problem you experienced?
- If the teacher were to read your paper right now, what would be the first thing the teacher would say about it?
- If the teacher were going to say something really nice about your draft, what would it be?
- Write a criticism of your draft. Imagine that your draft is in the hands of a critical English teacher. What would that teacher write?
- On the basis of the comments you've already received from your teacher, or your classmates, what changes do you intend to make when rewriting?
- List three important details in your paper.
- Look at your opening sentence. On a scale from 1 (lowest) to 10 (highest), what score would you give it?
- If you had something to add to this paper, what would it be?
- If you had to cut something, what would it be?
- What do you need to do to your paper between now and the day it's due? How long will that take?

(Whitlock 1984: 3)

Teacher feedback. This may take place at several stages during the writing process, rather than at the end of the process, where it no longer serves any useful purpose. The teacher may comment on quickwrites, rough drafts, and peer feedback, for example.

Checklists. Students may have short checklists, drawing their attention to specific features of sentence, paragraph, or text organization that they should attend to in revising.

Conclusions

Current approaches to the teaching of writing in a second or foreign language appear to be more effective than earlier product-focused approaches because they allow the learner to explore and develop a personal approach to writing. However, any attempt to reduce the teaching of writing to a system or set of formulas, or to turn the process approach into a "method" with prescribed techniques and practices, should be avoided. The effective writing teacher is not one who has developed a "method" for the teaching of writing, but one who can create an effective environment for learning, in which novice writers feel comfortable about writing and can explore the nature of writing – and in so doing discover their own strengths and weaknesses as writers. Throughout this process, roles of teachers and learners and patterns of interactions between them will have to be constantly negotiated. An understanding of the nature of written discourse and the characteristics of effective writing as well as an understanding of the strategies successful writers employ can guide the teacher in this process. The writing teacher is thus both a resource person for the novice writer and an investigator of the learners' writing processes, and this creates both the challenges and the rewards of teaching writing.

Discussion topics and activities

1. Do you consider yourself to be a good writer? What difficulties do you have with writing? How similar or different are your difficulties to those of nonnative writers?
2. Examine the list of differences between skilled and unskilled writers in the Appendix. How does the information in this list compare with the information from question 1?
3. Examine a piece of written discourse. What kinds of differences between written and spoken language are illustrated in the text?
4. Write a short description of a landscape (e.g., the view from your school window or a view of the school campus). Then reread the list of decisions writers must make when describing a landscape on page 102. How did you deal with these decisions in your description?
5. Examine an ESL composition text. What is its principal focus? To what extent does it address "product" and "process" issues?
6. Prepare a set of questions you could use to interview a writing teacher. Your questions should help you determine the teacher's approach to the teaching of writing, the kinds of activities employed, and how the teacher deals with issues of product and process. Then interview two teachers and compare their approaches to the teaching of writing. How do they see their role as writing teachers? What do they see the main problems in teaching writing to be?
7. Make arrangements to observe a writing teacher's class. First interview the teacher using the questions you prepared in question 6. Then observe the class. How does the teacher deal with issues of product and process in the class? How effective is the teacher's approach to the class, in your opinion, and why?
8. In groups select a writing assignment for a second or foreign language class, then prepare a lesson plan that addresses both product and process dimensions of writing.

Appendix: Differences between skilled and unskilled writers

1. Rehearsing and pre-writing behaviors

   Skilled writers
   Spend time thinking about the task and planning how they will approach it; gather and organize information.
   Have a variety of different strategies to help them, e.g. notetaking, reading, making lists.

   Unskilled writers
   Spend little time on planning.
   May start off confused about the task.
   Have few planning and organizing strategies available.

2. Drafting and writing behaviors

   Skilled writers
   Use information and ideas derived from rehearsing to trigger writing.
   Take time to let ideas develop.
   Get ideas onto paper quickly and fluently.
   Have sufficient language resources available (e.g. grammar, vocabulary) to enable them to concentrate on meaning rather than form.
   Spend time reviewing what they write, to allow for what they have written to trigger new ideas.
   Do most of their reviewing at the sentence or paragraph level.
   Know how to use reviewing to solve composing problems.
   Use reviewing to trigger planning.
   Refer back to rehearsing data to maintain focus and to trigger further writing.
   Are primarily concerned with higher levels of meaning.

   Unskilled writers.
   Begin the task immediately.
   Refer to the task or topic to trigger writing.
   Have limited language resources available and therefore quickly become concerned with language matters.
   Spend little time reviewing what they have produced.
   Review only short segments of text.
   Don't use reviewing to solve composing problems.
   Do not have access to rehearsing data.
   Concerned primarily with vocabulary choice and sentence formation.

Reprinted by permission of Ronald E. Lapp from "The process approach to writing: towards a curriculum for international students," 1984 master's thesis, available as a Working Paper from the Department of English as a Second Language, University of Hawaii.

3. Revising behaviors

Skilled writers
Make fewer formal changes at the surface level.
Use revisions successfully to clarify meanings.
Make effective revisions which change the direction and focus of the text.
Revise at all levels (lexical, sentence, discourse).
Add, delete, substitute, and reorder when revising.
Review and revise throughout the composing process.
Often pause for reviewing and revising during rewriting the first draft.
Revising does not interfere with the progress, direction, and control of the writing process.
Are not bothered by temporary confusions arising during the revising process.
Use revision process to generate new content and trigger need for further revision.

Unskilled writers
Make many formal changes at the surface level.
Revisions do not always clarify meanings.
Do not make major revisions in the direction or focus of the text.
Revise primarily at lexical and sentence level.
Do not make effective use of additions, deletions, substitutions, and reorderings.
Make most revisions only during writing the first draft.
Do not pause for reviewing while copying the first draft.
Revising interferes with the composing process.
Bothered by the confusion associated with revising, thus reducing the desire to revise.
Use revision process primarily to correct grammar, spelling, punctuation, vocabulary.

7 The teacher as self-observer: self-monitoring in teacher development

The classroom practices of language teachers are of interest to many different people. Program administrators and supervisors are interested in knowing whether the teacher's instructional practices are relevant to the program's goals and objectives. Students are interested in knowing whether the activities and experiences the teacher provides are helping them develop their language skills. And researchers are interested in studying the nature of the discourse teachers use in classrooms and the interactional structure of lessons. But those with the greatest interest in knowing what teachers do in classrooms are teachers themselves. All teachers want to know what kind of teachers they are and how well they are doing. A supervisor's evaluations and students' grades are ways of assessing this, but a more direct source of information for teachers is regular observation of their own teaching. Although few language teachers avail themselves of this resource on a regular basis, self-monitoring has much to recommend it as a component of the teacher's ongoing professional development.

What is self-monitoring?

Self-monitoring or self-observation refers to a systematic approach to the observation, evaluation, and management of one's own behavior (Armstrong and Frith 1984), for the purposes of achieving a better understanding and control over one's behavior. In everyday life, people often make use of self-monitoring, such as when a shopper uses a shopping list to guide and restrict purchases during shopping, or when a person writes a daily personal diary and periodically reviews it to monitor progress in attaining personal goals. In language teaching, self-monitoring refers to the teacher making a record of a lesson, either in the form of a written account or an audio or video recording of a lesson, and using the information obtained as a source of feedback on his or her teaching. Self-monitoring is an approach to teacher evaluation that complements, rather than replaces, other forms of assessment, such as feedback from students, peers, or supervisors.

Why use self-monitoring?

There are several good reasons for the use of self-monitoring by teachers.

(1) For most teachers, the amount of time they spend in professional training is relatively short in comparison to the length of their teaching careers. But teacher training programs should mark the beginning – not the end – of professional development. In order to improve performance over time, however, teachers need feedback on what they do and how well they do it. Self-monitoring is a means of obtaining such feedback and is hence a key ingredient in a teacher's continuing growth and development as a professional.

(2) Self-monitoring provides an opportunity for teachers to reflect critically on their teaching. Reflection is acknowledged to be a key component of many models of teacher development. The skills of self-inquiry and critical thinking are seen as central for continued professional growth (Zeichner 1982). Self-monitoring enables teachers to move from a level where they may be guided largely by impulse, intuition, or routine to a level where their actions are guided by reflection and critical thinking.

(3) Self-monitoring can help narrow the gap between teachers' imagined view of their own teaching and reality – a gap that is often considerable, according to research (Swaffar et al. 1982; Long and Sato 1983). Swaffar et al. (1982), for example, found that although teachers may be using different methodological approaches and may think they are therefore employing different classroom practices, on closer examination their actual classroom practices reflect a pool of common instructional behaviors. Self-monitoring can hence help teachers better understand their own instructional processes.

(4) Self-monitoring shifts the responsibility for initiating improvement in teaching practices from an outsider, such as a supervisor, to teachers themselves (although it does not obviate the need for objective evaluation of teaching). It enables teachers to arrive at their own judgments as to what works and what does not work in their classrooms.

What can be learned from self-monitoring?

Luft (1969) categorizes four types of information about teacher behavior that teachers can examine through self-assessment: information concerning the open self, the secret self, the blind self, and the undiscovered self.

The open self refers to information about a teacher's behavior that is known to the teacher and to others – that is, information that the teacher is willing and able to share with others. The challenge for the teacher is to go beyond the open self and explore the secret, blind, and hidden selves when looking for areas for improvement.

The secret self refers to information known to the teacher but not to others. For example, a teacher may be experiencing difficulty in implementing a new set of course guidelines but is unwilling to share this uneasiness with colleagues in case they judge him or her to be incompetent.

The blind self refers to information known to others but not to the teacher. For example, a teacher may unknowingly reinforce certain sex-role stereotypes without realizing it, even though this is recognized both by students and colleagues.

The hidden self refers to information about a teacher's behavior that is unknown to both the teacher and to others within the school environment (Iwanicki and McEachern 1984). For example, neither the teacher nor others in the school may understand why the teacher is achieving less-than-expected results with a set of new materials. Through self-monitoring the teacher seeks to find out what the critical factors are that could explain the problem.

How is self-monitoring carried out?

There are three major approaches available to self-monitoring in teaching – through personal reflection, self-reporting, and audio or video recordings of a lesson.

Personal reflection

The simplest approach to self-monitoring is through the use of a diary or journal in which the teacher makes an honest and open report of what happened in a lesson. Bailey (1990) defines a diary study as

a first-person account of a language learning or teaching experience, documented through regular, candid entries in a personal journal and then analyzed for recurring patterns or salient events.

While diary studies may seem to be an anecdotal and subjective approach to collecting data, it should be remembered that researchers in disciplines such as anthropology, ethnography, and linguistics have for many years made succcessful use of diary reports as a way of exploring phenomena that are often difficult to investigate in other ways.

The goal in making a diary account of a lesson is to write recollections of a lesson in as much detail as possible (Bailey 1983). Extensive written notes are made as soon as possible after the lesson is taught. Alternatively, the teacher may record his or her recollections with a tape recorder. Both the events themselves and the writer's personal feelings and reactions to them are recorded in detail. The diary may be used to record several kinds of information. The most frequent entries will be recollections of lessons that were taught and events that took place during a lesson. These may be entered more or less verbatim. Reactions to classroom events and interpretations of what went on in a lesson should also be recorded. In addition, ideas for future analysis and reminders of needed actions can be noted. But keeping a diary account of teaching should be accompanied by regular review and analysis of what has been recorded if it is to serve as a source of professional growth.

There are several advantages to reflecting on one's teaching through a diary record in this way. A diary allows a person to explore information and thoughts that may not be accessible in other ways. By later reviewing what was written, things that may not have been obvious when they were first recorded may become apparent. In addition, the mere act of writing about one's teaching experiences often serves to initiate insights into the nature and meaning of those experiences. The writing process thus serves to trigger critical reflection. Deene (cited in Bailey 1990) comments on the benefits of conducting a diary study:

The study showed the role the diary played in defining a personal philosophy of teaching and it reflected problems with building an image of what a classroom looks like and what the teacher's roles are in project-based learning...
Keeping a diary helped me very much in clarifying my thoughts and feelings about learning and my way of handling problems that came forth from doing real learning.

Perhaps the most famous example of the use of a diary as an aid to reflection on teaching is Sylvia Ashton-Warner's *Teacher* (1965) – an account of her experiences with Maori children in New Zealand elementary schools. In the process she created a book that has become a classic in the literature on the teaching of reading.

This afternoon marks the beginning of composition. Word composition. Writing. The first wall between one liver and another. Putting thoughts in writing for the other instead of the direct route of speech or touch. I'm both gratified and sad. Talkers and touchers are never lonely but writers are. Here is the beginning of loneliness. Should I be glad because my children are voluntarily composing sentences for the first time? One Twinnie is writing on the blackboard about the story: "The fish is jumped. The fish is swimming. The little fish is in the sea. The fish he have no leg." Ah well I can't stop civilization. A picture springs into the world behind my eyes of a Maori marae [ceremonial meeting house] of the past with the tattooed, impassioned speakers. The direct vital communication at all times. (p. 117)

In practicum courses, novice teachers also find diary accounts a useful way to explore their experiences. The following are examples of entries made by a student teacher from China, who was completing a practicum with the author. Near the beginning of her practice teaching experience she writes of one lesson in a conversation course:

I liked my pacing generally today, but I found that I did not give the students enough time to practice on one task before going on to another. I was also too nervous to function well. I made more grammatical mistakes than I should have. The students were very helpful and cooperative. Today's tasks were a little too easy for most of the students. I should have prepared something more challenging.

A week later she writes:

Today I found myself using a lot of teaching strategies that I used to use in China. I tended to explain too much, tended to make the class teacher-centered. Next time I teach, I will pay special attention to this. I must try to remember that these students come to class to practice speaking English – not to listen to me.

She soon begins to note an improvement in her performance, and at the same time records points for future action:

I felt much more confident today. The way I presented the lesson was much more challenging for the students than last time. The pacing was better too. I felt that the students were all involved in the lesson. However I did not handle the group-work exercise well. My directions were not clear and some of the students did not understand the exercise. I didn't give them enough time to work on it either.

After a particularly frustrating lesson she writes:

Sometimes I ask myself "Can anyone be a teacher?" "Does anyone know how to teach?" My answer is Yes and No. Sometimes I feel that teaching is the hardest job in the world. Many jobs require only your hands and brain, but teaching requires much more. Hands, brain, eyes and mouth. A good teacher is someone who knows how to handle these parts beautifully at the same time. Sometimes I think I am not cut out to be a teacher, because I do not possess what a good teacher has: logical thinking, well-organized talking, spontaneous response. Sometimes I decide that I will become a good teacher if I know how to learn, to observe, to practice. "Where there is a will, there is a way."

But a week later she observes:

I felt so good about my teaching today. Everything went well. I could tell the students were on task. I found that my ability to give clear explanations has improved a lot. In today's class I did not find any cases where students could not understand my instructions as in my earlier classes.

And later she revises an earlier impression of her teaching:

I used to think I was not cut out to be a teacher, because I don't possess some of the important characteristics that a good teacher should have...

However, after today's teaching, I began to think my earlier conclusion about my teaching was a little unfair. I didn't expect that today's lesson would turn out to be so successful. Both my students and I functioned very well.

For student teachers as well as experienced teachers, a diary account can hence serve as one source of information on what happens in the classroom and can assist in the interpretation of classroom events.

Self-reporting

Self-reporting is another approach to gathering data on one's own teaching practices, a procedure that is said to be both cost effective and efficient. Self-reporting involves completing an inventory or checklist in which the teacher indicates which teaching practices were used within a lesson or within a specified time period and how often they were employed. As many as one hundred items may be included on the self-report inventory. The inventory may be completed individually or in group sessions. In view of the observation that teachers' perceptions of how they teach may not coincide with an observer's perception of their teaching, the reliability of teacher self-reports might be presumed to be low. In the past, this was often found to be the case (Good and Brophy 1973). But reliability can be increased by using self-report inventories that focus on specific instructional practices. When questions have a very specific focus, comparisons of the accuracy of teacher self-reports with observation reports made by outside observers have revealed agreement around 75% of the time (Koziol and Burns 1985). Accuracy is found to increase when teachers focus on the teaching of specific skills in a particular classroom context and when the self-report instrument is carefully constructed to reflect a wide range of potential teaching practices and behaviors.

Self-reporting allows teachers to make a regular assessment of what they are doing in the classroom. They can check to see to what extent their assumptions about their own teaching are reflected in their actual teaching practices. For example, a teacher could use self-reporting to find out:

the kinds of teaching activities being used regularly
whether all of the program's goals are being addressed
the degree to which personal goals for a class are being met
the kinds of activities that seem to work well or not to work well

Koziol and Burns (1985) found that student teachers in English classes who completed self-report inventories on a regular basis tended to be "more realistic about their own teaching and more concrete in the questions they ask of supervisors" (p. 119). Appendix 1 presents a sample of a self-report inventory that focuses on instructional practices in the teaching of grammar (Koziol and Call 1986). It illustrates how inventories can be constructed that focus on specific skills in particular content areas. Koziol and Call report that teachers seem to be much more able to characterize their instruction accurately when items related to instruction are cast directly in terms of the subject matter being taught.

Appendix 2 is a self-observation checklist developed by Christison and Bassano (1984). This is not designed to provide a retrospective account of the instructional practices used in a given lesson or time period but is intended more to stimulate critical and focused reflection on the teacher's philosophy or teaching style. Pak (1985) contains a collection of self-report questionnaires that deal with techniques for presenting vocabulary in an ESL lesson (see Appendix 3).

Recording lessons

For many aspects of teaching, audio or video recording of lessons provides a more reliable record of what actually happened than diaries or self-reports. Although many useful insights can be gained from diaries and self-reports, they cannot capture the moment-to-moment processes of teaching. Many events happen simultaneously in a classroom, and some aspects of a lesson cannot be recalled. It would be of little value, for example, to attempt to recall the proportion of Yes/No questions to Wh-questions a teacher used during a lesson, or to estimate the degree to which teacher time was shared among higher- and lower-ability students. Many significant classroom events may not have been observed by the teacher, let alone remembered – hence the need to supplement diaries or self-reports with recordings of actual lessons.

The simplest way of recording a lesson is to place a tape recorder where it can capture the exchanges that occur in class. With the microphone placed on the teacher's table, much of the teacher's language can be recorded as well as the exchanges of many of the students in the class. Pak (1985) recommends recording for a one- or two-week period and then randomly selecting one cassette for closer analysis. This recording could be used as the basis for an initial assessment. If video facilities are available, the teacher can request to have a lesson recorded, or perhaps students themselves can be assigned this responsibility. A thirty-minute recording usually provides more than sufficient data for analysis. The goal is to capture as much of the interaction of the class as possible, both teacher to class and student to student. Once the initial novelty wears off, both students and teacher accept the presence of the technician with the camera, and the class proceeds with minimum disruption.

McLaughlin (1985: 155–6) cites a striking example of how a teacher discovered information about her blind and hidden selves through examining a video of her class.

The study was carried out in a kindergarten classroom in a Southern California community. The classroom was multilingual and multicultural. The target child ... was raised in Mexico by her grandmother and had no access to radio, puzzles, toys ... until she was brought to the US ... She was a quiet, well behaved 6 year old child, but tested very poorly. In fact, by mid-year, the teacher had decided to retain her in kindergarten for another year. The teacher rarely called on her in whole- or small-group discussions, out of fear of humiliating her in front of her peers. The teacher was concerned that Lupita not develop a negative attitude toward school and toward herself.

In her interactions with her peers, Lupita displayed excellent oral Spanish. Having observed this, the researcher decided to videotape Lupita as she performed and interacted outside of the teacher's awareness during "free time." The tape showed Lupita helping other children, being asked for help by them, and in general acting as a leader and a teacher for her peers. When the teacher viewed this she was quite taken aback. She admitted she had evaluated the child on the basis of the child's history and home background and because she had initially tested so poorly. Subsequently Lupita "spurted" and was able to enter the first grade the following year ...

The videotape had, in effect, made Lupita visible to the teacher. Closer analysis of the videotape had shown that when Lupita came into the teacher's line of vision, she invariably did something to appear busy; she focussed on some chore and acted as if the teacher were not there. This interaction pattern enabled her to remain invisible to the teacher. Once the teacher's behavior toward her changed, however, she modified her own behavior.

Although simply viewing a video of a class can reveal a great deal about a teacher's blind or hidden self, as this example demonstrates, in order to make effective use of the rich source of information such recordings contain, it is sometimes necessary to be able to conceptualize the nature of classroom behavior and classroom interaction. Studies have shown that merely viewing tapes of one's own lessons does not always improve teachers' understanding of their own teaching (Good and Brophy 1973). What is needed is a systematic and objective way to explore the information contained in classroom recordings. In order to do this, it is necessary both to have an idea of what one is looking for and to keep an open mind toward unexpected discoveries that will arise from the process of viewing and thinking about the recordings.

What to look for in lessons

A number of aspects of classroom life can be examined when reviewing diary entries, self-reports, or recordings of lessons. One set of behaviors relates to the teacher's handling of classroom management, teacher–student interaction, grouping, structuring, and tasks. The following are some of the relevant issues (see Chapter 2 for further discussion).

The language teaching matrix

Classroom management
What rules govern classroom behavior?
How are expectations for positive and negative classroom behavior communicated and reinforced?
How are problem students dealt with?
How is attention to instructional tasks maintained?

Teacher–student interaction
How much teacher-to-student communication occurs in a lesson?
How much student-to-teacher interaction is there?
To what extent does the lesson engage the learners?
How is student attention and interest maintained?
What turn-taking patterns are observed?

Grouping
What grouping arrangements are employed?
Is there a clear relationship between grouping patterns and instructional goals?
Are grouping arrangements effective?
How are groups established? Do students always work with the same partners or in the same groups?

Structuring
How clearly are the goals of activities communicated to students?
Is there a clear relationship between different activities within a lesson?
Is there any sense of development within a lesson, or is it merely a succession of unrelated activities, the logic for which is not apparent?
What kind of opening and closing does the lesson have?

Tasks
What kinds of tasks or activities are employed during a lesson?
What kinds of demands do these tasks create?
Is the pacing of tasks adequate? Is too little time spent on some tasks and too much on others?
For how much of the lesson are students actively engaged in learning tasks? How much of the lesson is spent on procedural and other noninstructional matters?
Are the tasks interesting and challenging to students?
How does the teacher give feedback on task performance?
How effective is the teacher's feedback?

Teaching resources
What teaching aids are used?

How effective is the teacher's use of aids, such as overhead projector, blackboard, or audiocassette or videocassette player?

Questions like these can be asked about any lesson. There are other questions, however, that will depend on the content of a particular lesson, and will reflect assumptions about the nature of second language instruction in specific content areas. Such questions will vary according to whether the teacher is teaching listening, speaking, reading, or writing, and what aspects of each skill are being taught and at what level. In a course dealing with speaking skills, for example, relevant areas of investigation would include the following:

Classroom interactions
What kinds of interactions occur between teacher and class, and among students themselves? What "functions" are employed during the lesson?

Opportunities for speaking
How much opportunity is provided for students to speak? What is the ratio of teacher talk to student talk?

Quality of input
What kind of input is the teacher's speech providing? Is the teacher using a natural speaking style or a classroom "foreigner talk"?
To what extent does the teacher use translation or the native tongue in teaching?

Communicativeness
Are opportunities provided for real communication in the classroom? To what extent?
Is there "negotiation of meaning" in the classroom?
To what extent is accuracy or fluency the focus of activities?

Questions
What kind of questioning patterns are used?
Are questions distributed between teachers and students and among different students in the class?

Feedback
How does the teacher correct errors and answer requests for clarification?
How are communication breakdowns dealt with?

Although diary accounts and self-reports may provide tentative answers to some of these questions, many of them can be answered only by examining recordings of lessons. Analyzing recordings of classroom lessons raises special problems, however. Let us look at some of the issues involved and how they can be addressed.

Looking at recordings of lessons

The fundamental problem that confronts anyone looking at recordings of lessons arises from the nature of classroom events themselves: They are very complex phenomena involving many different kinds of interactions and processes. Every lesson contains simultaneous occurrences of multiple events, many of which are unpredictable. While some aspects of classroom life can be observed directly, others are more abstract and need to be inferred, if they can be understood at all. For example, suppose that a teacher was interested in looking at an aspect of classroom management, such as determining the rules used to control student behavior in the classroom. How would the teacher know what to look for? What would count as an instance of use of a rule and what would not? The problem is that "rules" cannot always be observed directly. They have to be inferred. However, if the teacher was interested in looking at an aspect of grouping, such as the time spent on different grouping arrangements during a lesson, this would be an easier matter to determine.

In order to make the task of identifying different features of lessons easier, it is often necessary to operationalize the categories or behaviors that are being observed. For example, if a teacher wanted to find out the extent to which he or she was being fair in dealings with students, the teacher might look for the amount of time spent with different kinds of students during a typical lesson. Six students could be targeted for observation in a recording of a lesson – two students the teacher liked, two students the teacher felt neutral about, and two students the teacher disliked. Then the number of times the teacher interacted with each set of students during a lesson could be counted.

Some teacher educators train teachers to code tapes of their lessons using observational forms. The advantage of structured observation instruments is that they enable the observer to focus on a specific kind of classroom behavior, and to focus on one thing at a time. A tape can be listened to once, focusing on one aspect of the lesson, and then listened to a second time focusing on a different aspect of the lesson. The forms focus on specific observable behaviors and hence can be coded in real time. High reliability can be attained after a short period of training. Appendix 4 presents examples of observational forms from Good and Brophy (1973). The first observational form is used to identify the ways in which teachers end a lesson or group activity. Each instance of a specific strategy the teacher employs is noted as it is observed. The second observational form deals with the amount of time the teacher spends on different tasks and activities during a lesson, and enables the observer to measure the amount of time-on-task during a lesson. The third observational form codes different kinds of responses to student questions.

In the field of second language teaching, teacher educators and researchers have developed many different coding systems for use in looking at the interactional, discourse, and linguistic structure of second language classroom events. Faneslow (1977) has developed a system known as FOCUS (Foci for Observing Communications Used in Settings), which can be used to code many different dimensions of lessons. The FOCUS system has been widely used in TESOL teacher training at Columbia University. It distinguishes between the source and the target of an act of communication, and identifies the purpose of the communication, the medium of communication used, the way in which a given medium is used to communicate content, and what area of content is communicated in the lesson. Other observation systems and their use in second language classrooms are described by Allen, Fröhlich, and Spada (1985) and Bailey (1983). These observation systems are designed to assist teachers to think about a lesson objectively and to develop a metalanguage for describing their own teaching. They are useful to the extent that they function as means to an end rather than ends in themselves, and are more useful for analyzing some aspects of teaching than others. Hence a variety of ways of approaching the analysis of classroom lessons is often needed.

Guidelines for self-monitoring

Self-monitoring, whether it be through diary accounts, self-reports, or recording of lessons, is recommended as a practical tool for occasional but regular use. In order to apply self-monitoring techniques effectively, the following guidelines are suggested for teachers.

1. Decide what aspect of your teaching you are interested in learning more about or you wish to improve. What are your strong and weak points? Are there areas of your teaching that you would like to know more about? Find out where you are in your professional development by reflecting on problems you may be having with specific aspects of your teaching, by reviewing supervisors' comments and student evaluations, by inviting a colleague to view your teaching in order to offer suggestions, or by reviewing current issues in the literature and considering how they relate to your own teaching. You may discover that you are a poor classroom manager, that you make poor use of the blackboard, or that you spend too much class time on nonessentials. There

129

are virtually no areas of teaching that cannot be improved through self-monitoring.

2. Narrow your choices to those that seem most important to you. In order to make effective use of self-monitoring techniques it is necessary to focus on one area at a time.

3. Develop a plan of action to address the specific problem area you have identified. Which of your teaching behaviors will you attempt to change? What effects will these changes in your behavior have on student behaviors? For example, a videotape of your lesson reveals that there is very little student participation in your lessons. Students occasionally answer questions when called upon but seldom initiate questions or discussions. Many students say nothing at all during a whole lesson, leaving two or three more active students to do most of the talking. You conclude that this is largely because you seldom give students the opportunity to interact either with you or with other students. Most of your classroom activities are teacher directed and there is very little use of student-directed activities, such as pair or small-group tasks. You decide on a change in your instructional practices – you will spend less time on the class text and make more use of supplementary group activities. You will also monitor student interaction during group tasks to assess the extent to which you have managed to bring about an increase in student participation in lessons.

4. Draw up a time frame to carry out your goals. You may decide to give yourself a week or two to try out new approaches and then monitor yourself to discover the effectiveness of the strategies you have chosen. Decide on the self-monitoring procedures you will use. Check your self-report forms or the recording of your lesson to see if you have been successful in modifying the behaviors you wanted to change.

An example of the effectiveness of this approach was demonstrated by a student teacher who wanted to improve how she gave feedback to students on errors. On listening to a recording of one of her lessons in a conversation class, she discovered that she was providing confusing feedback to students on their errors. Sometimes she would correct a serious error of grammar or pronunciation by pretending that she had not understood what the student had said, prompting the student to repeat the sentence several times. However this seldom resulted in a self-correction by the student. For example,

S: The weekend...I go...to a party.
T: Sorry?
S: The weekend I go to party.

At other times the teacher noticed that she repeated the student's error:

S: The weekend I go to a party.

T: Go to a party?
S: Yes, I go to party.

She decided to implement a simple error correction strategy and to attempt to use it consistently. In future, when the student made a serious error of grammar or pronunciation, she would intervene and provide the correct form prefaced with, "Say . . . " For example:

S: The weekend I go to a party.
T: Say "went to a party."
S: The weekend I went to party.

Two weeks later the teacher recorded another lesson. On checking she found that she was no longer providing inconsistent feedback on errors and as a consequence was providing feedback that was less disruptive to her students' communicative efforts.

Another teacher – a nonnative speaker of English – wanted to increase the amount of English he was using in the classroom. To do this he first investigated how much he used his native tongue (Japanese) during his teaching and for what purposes he was using it. He checked three tapes recorded at different times over a two-week period and first listened to them just to determine the proportion of English to Japanese he was using. It was about 70% English, 30% Japanese. He then listened to the tapes again to find out the purposes for which he was using Japanese. He found he was using Japanese for two main purposes: classroom management and giving feedback. He then drew up a plan to reduce the amount of Japanese he was using for these two purposes. He first consulted a guide to the use of English in the classroom (Willis 1981) and familiarized himself with English expressions that could be used for classroom management and feedback. He wrote out a set of expressions and strategies on 3" by 5" cards, and put these in a conspicuous place on his table. These served not only to remind him of his plan but also helped him remember some of the expressions he wanted to use. Each day he would place a different card on top of the pile. He then continued recording his lessons and after a few weeks checked his tapes. His use of Japanese had declined considerably.

Conclusions

Self-monitoring has many useful applications in language teaching. The best way to determine whether self-monitoring has anything to offer is to try it on a small scale, using the experience to assess its use on a more regular basis. Many teachers have found that self-monitoring techniques give them a far greater insight into their own teaching than more traditional forms of teacher assessment, and are at the same time a simple but effective way of improving the management and understanding of their own teaching.

Discussion topics and activities

1. Provide examples of aspects of a teacher's behavior that relate to
   a) the open self
   b) the secret self
   c) the blind self
   d) the hidden self.
2. Prepare a self-report checklist that could be used in connection with a class you are teaching or taking. Make your checklist as specific as possible. If possible, try out the checklist and discuss your findings with other students.
3. In groups, prepare a self-report checklist that could be used by a teacher teaching a basic-level course in listening, speaking, reading, or writing.
4. Make arrangements to record a lesson you teach (or another teacher's lesson) with a tape recorder. Then listen to the tape. What aspects of the lesson were you able to capture? What did you miss? How useful was your recording in capturing the major aspects of what went on during the lesson?
5. Select one of the aspects of lessons discussed on pages 126–127. Look at the questions associated with each topic. Expand or revise the list of questions and produce a set of questions you would like to focus on in a lesson. Then videotape one of your classes or that of another teacher. Examine the lesson using the questions you prepared.
6. Prepare a coded observation form that could be used in observing a videorecording of a lesson. Focus on the aspect of the lesson you looked at in question 5. Now view the video again, using your coding form. How useful was your form? What did you learn about the lesson from this activity that you might otherwise have been unaware of?
7. Discuss the advantages and disadvantages of the three approaches to self-monitoring presented in this chapter: diaries, self-reports, and recording lessons. Which approach would you feel most comfortable with? Why?

Appendix 1: Sample self-report inventory

This inventory focuses on instructional practices in teaching grammar.

Name _____ Week of _____

Class (language) _____ Level _____ Period ____

This is an inventory that asks you to identify how many times you used a given teaching practice in a particular class in a given week. Please use this key in responding to the following statements relating to different aspects of grammar presentations.

0 = Never   This is something that I did not do in this particular class this week.

1 = Infrequently This is something that I did once this week in this class.

2 = Sometimes   This is something that I did two or three times this week in this class.

3 = Regularly   This is something that I did four or five times this week in this class.

In presenting a grammar teaching point for the first time I:

_____ 1. presented the teaching point both orally and with visual aids.

_____ 2. used pictures and diagrams to convey the meaning of the teaching point.

_____ 3. presented the teaching point indirectly in the context of spoken language, but did not formally teach it.

_____ 4. presented the teaching point indirectly in the context of written language, but did not formally teach it.

_____ 5. presented the teaching point indirectly in the context of spoken language and pointed it out to the students.

_____ 6. presented the teaching point indirectly in the context of written language and pointed it out to the students.

_____ 7. presented the teaching point using only the target language.

_____ 8. reviewed with the students relevant, previously presented grammatical structures.

_____ 9. gave the students several examples of the teaching point, and guided them in discovering the grammatical rule.

_____ 10. gave the students several examples of the teaching point, before supplying them with the grammatical rule.

_____ 11. translated examples of the teaching point to be certain that the students understood.

Reprinted with permission from S. M. Koziol and M. E. Call, 1986, "Constructing and using teacher self-report inventories," paper presented at the TESOL Convention in Anaheim (March).

_____ 12. assisted the students in participating in a target language conversation, then drew the teaching point from the language that the students themselves had generated.

_____ 13. spoke only in the target language, but modified the structure, vocabulary, and speed so that the students could understand easily.

_____ 14. did not focus on grammar in the teaching of language.

_____ 15. based new teaching points on previously presented grammatical structures.

_____ 16. gave only one example of the teaching point and did it orally.

_____ 17. embedded the teaching point in a command designed to elicit a nonverbal response from the students.

_____ 18. relied on gestures and mime to convey the meaning of the teaching point.

_____ 19. drew the teaching point from dialogues that the students had memorized.

_____ 20. explained the teaching point in English.

_____ 21. conducted oral drills on the teaching point before presenting it formally.

_____ 22. wrote the grammatical rule on the board/overhead before beginning to explain it.

_____ 23. gave the students the general grammatical rule, then wrote examples of the rule on the board/overhead.

_____ 24. allowed students to look at the explanation in their textbooks while I was presenting the teaching point.

_____ 25. had the students read a grammar explanation in their texts before I presented it in class.

Appendix 2: Teacher self-observation checklist

Thoughtfully consider each statement. Rate yourself in the following way:

3 • Excellent   2 • Good   1 • Needs improvement   0 • Not applicable

Write your rating in the blanks provided. When you have finished, give over-all consideration to the various areas.

I. Learning Environment

   A. Relationship to students

      ____ 1. I establish good eye contact with my class. I do not talk over their heads, to the blackboard or to just one individual.

      ____ 2. If I tend to teach predominantly to one area of the classroom, I am aware of this. I make a conscious effort at all times to pay attention to all students equally.

      ____ 3. I divide my students into small groups in an organized and prin-cipled manner. I recognize that these groups should differ in size and composition, varying with the objective of the group activity.

   B. The Classroom

      ____ 1. I arrange the seating in my class to suit the class activity for the day.

      ____ 2. I consider the physical comfort of the room such as heat and light.

      ____ 3. When I need special materials or equipment, I have them set up before the class begins.

   C. Presentation

      ____ 1. My handwriting on the blackboard and charts is legible from all locations in the classroom. It is large enough to accommodate students with vision impairments.

      ____ 2. I speak loudly enough to be heard in all parts of the classroom and I enunciate clearly.

      ____ 3. I vary the exercises in class, alternating rapid and slow paced activities to keep up maximum interest level in the class.

      ____ 4. I am prepared to give a variety of explanations, models or de-scriptions, understanding that one explanation may not be suffi-cient for all students.

      ____ 5. I help the students form working principles and generalizations.

      ____ 6. Students use new skills or concepts long enough so that they are retained and thus future application is possible.

      ____ 7. I plan for "thinking time" time for my students so they can or-ganize their thoughts and plan what they are going to say or do.

Reprinted with permission from M. A. Christison and S. Bassano, "Teacher self-obser-vation," *TESOL Newsletter* 18, 4 (1984):17–19.

D. Culture and Adjustment

____ 1. I am aware that cultural differences affect the learning situation.

____ 2. I keep the cultural background(s) of my students in mind when planning daily activities and am aware of culture misunderstandings which might arise from the activities I choose.

____ 3. I work for an atmosphere of understanding and mutual respect.

II. The Individuals

A. Physical Health

____ 1. I know which students have visual or aural impairments, and have seated them as close to my usual teaching position as possible.

____ 2. I am aware that a student's attention span varies from day to day depending on mental and physical health and outside distractions. I pace my class activities to accommodate the strengths. I don't continue with an activity which may exhaust or bore them.

____ 3. I begin my class with a simple activity to wake the students up and get them working together.

____ 4. I am sensitive to individual students who have bad days. I don't press a student who is incapable of performing at the usual level.

____ 5. I try to challenge students who are at their best.

____ 6. If I am having a bad day and feel it might affect my normal teaching style, I let my students know so there is no misunderstanding about my feelings for them.

B. Self-concepts

____ 1. I treat my students with the same respect that I expect them to show me.

____ 2. I plan "one-centered" activities which give all students an opportunity at some point to feel important and accepted.

____ 3. I like to teach and have a good time teaching – on most days.

C. Aptitude and Perception

____ 1. I am aware that my students learn differently. Some students are visual-receptive, some are motor-receptive, and others are audio-receptive.

____ 2. My exercises are varied, some are visual, aural, oral and kinesthetic. I provide models, examples, and experiences to maximize learning in each of these areas.

____ 3. I know basic concepts in the memory process. When applicable, I make use of techniques such as backward buildup and association to aid students in rapid skill acquisition.

D. Reinforcement

____ 1. I tell students when they have done well, but I don't let praise become mechanical.

____ 2. I finish my class period in a way which will review the new concepts presented during the class period. My students can immediately evaluate their understanding of those concepts.

_____ 3. My tests are well-planned and produced.

_____ 4. I make my system of grading clear to my students so that there are no misunderstandings of expectations.

E. Development

_____ 1. I keep up to date on new techniques in the ESL profession by attending conferences and workshops and by reading pertinent professional articles and books.

_____ 2. I realize that there is no one right way to present any lesson. I try new ideas where and when they seem appropriate.

_____ 3. I observe other ESL teachers so that I can get other ideas and compare them to my own teaching style. I want to have several ideas for teaching any one concept.

III. The Activity

A. Interaction

_____ 1. I minimize my role in *conducting* the activities.

_____ 2. I organize the activities so they are suitable for *real* interaction among the students.

_____ 3. The activities maximize student involvement.

_____ 4. The activities promote spontaneity or experimentation on the part of the learner.

_____ 5. The activities generally transfer attention away from "self" and outward toward a "task."

_____ 6. The activities are organized to insure a high success rate, leaving enough room for error to make the activity challenging.

_____ 7. I am not overly concerned with error correction. I concentrate on what my students are saying (content).

B. Language

_____ 1. The activity is focused.

_____ 2. The content or the skill presented will be easily transferrable for use outside the class.

_____ 3. The activity is geared to the proficiency level of my class or slightly beyond.

_____ 4. The content of the activity is not too sophisticated for my students.

_____ 5. I make the content of the activity relevant and meaningful to my students' world.

Appendix 3: Self-report form for vocabulary teaching

Vocabulary

1. (a) How did you spend time on vocabulary?

    Incidentally (as words came up) ☐

    Planned ☐

    (b) List the vocabulary covered in the lesson.

    ....

    ....

    ....

    ....

2. (a) When introducing vocabulary did you move from the known to the unknown?
    (List examples)

    ....

    ....

    ....

    (b) Do you see how encouraging guessing of unknown terms could lead to greater effectiveness?

    ....

    ....

3. (a) Did you elicit vocabulary from the students, e.g. through prediction?
    (List examples)

    ....

    ....

    ....

    ....

Reprinted with permission from Janine Pak, *Find Out How You Teach*, National Curriculum Resource Centre, Adelaide, Australia, 1985.

Appendix 3: (*continued*)

(b) At any point could you have increased student input?

....

....

4. (a) What technique(s) did you use for clarification?

Giving examples ☐

Providing synonyms ☐

Use in context ☐

Visual aids ☐

Mime/gesture ☐

Other ☐

(b) Do you see any other way that you could have achieved greater clarity?

....

....

5. (a) Did you check understanding of meaning?
How?

....

....

(b) Could you have increased comprehension by such means as concept questions? (Questions that don't use what is being checked).

Can you list any you used/could have used?

....

....

6. (a) Did you pay attention to the pronunciation of new vocabulary?

Yes ☐

No ☐

Appendix 3: (*continued*)

(b) Do you see how this is beneficial?

....

....

7. (a) Did you provide opportunity for the students to

use ☐

practise
new vocabulary ☐

How?..

....

(b) Is there any other way you could have offered more practice?

....

....

8. (a) Was vocabulary integrated with other aspects of the lesson or was it treated in isolation?

....

....

(b) Would you make any changes in this next time?
Why?

....

....

9. (a) Did the students learn anything new?

....

(b) How do you know?

....

(c) Could you do anything to increase that learning?

....

Appendix 4: Structured observation form

This form describes how the teacher closes a lesson.

FORM 4.2. Evaluations After Lessons and Activities

USE: When teacher ends a lesson or group activity
PURPOSE: To see whether the teacher stresses learning or compliance in
making evaluations
When the teacher ends a lesson or group activity, code any summary
evaluations he or she makes about the group's performance during the activity.

BEHAVIOR CATEGORIES   CODES

1. Praises progress in specific terms; labels knowledge   1. _5_   26. ___
   or skills learned   2. _5_   27. ___
2. Criticizes performance or indicates weaknesses in   3. _9_   28. ___
   specific terms   4. ___   29. ___
3. Praises generally good performance, for doing   5. ___   30. ___
   well or knowing answers
4. Criticizes generally poor performance   6. ___   31. ___
   (doesn't detail the specifics)   7. ___   32. ___
5. Ambiguous general praise ("You were very good   8. ___   33. ___
   today.")   9. ___   34. ___
6. Ambiguous general criticism ("You weren't very   10. ___   35. ___
   good today.")
7. Praises good attention or good behavior   11. ___   36. ___
8. Criticizes poor attention or misbehavior   12. ___   37. ___
9. No general evaluations of performance were made   13. ___   38. ___
10. Other (specify)   14. ___   39. ___
NOTES: 15. ___   40. ___

Teacher uses stock phrase ("You were   16. ___   41. ___
really good today; I'm very pleased").   17. ___   42. ___
                                                    18. ___   43. ___
                                                    19. ___   44. ___
* 13 cut off by bell; might have praised   20. ___   45. ___
otherwise.
                                                    21. ___   46. ___
                                                    22. ___   47. ___
1= Homework Review   23. ___   48. ___
                                                    24. ___   49. ___
2= Division Facts Drill   25. ___   50. ___

3 = Board Work

The forms in this appendix are reprinted from T. L. Good and J. E. Brophy, *Looking in Classrooms*, 4th ed., pp. 164, 170, and 209. Copyright ©1987 by Harper & Row, Publishers, Inc. Reprinted by permission of the publisher.

Appendix 4: (*continued*)

This form describes how much time the teacher spends on different class-room activities.

FORM 4.6. Teacher's Use of Time

USE: *Whenever activities are introduced or changed*
PURPOSE: *To see if the teacher spends time primarily on activities related to teaching and learning*
Record starting time and elapsed time for the following teacher activities (when more than one activity is going on, record the one in which the teacher is involved). Totals for the day are entered in the blanks in the lower left corner of the page.

BEHAVIOR CATEGORIES
1. Daily rituals (pledge, prayer, song, collection, roll, washroom, etc.)
2. Transitions between activities
3. Whole class lessons or tests (academic curriculum)
4. Small group lessons or tests (academic curriculum)
5. Going around the room checking seatwork or small group assignments
6. Doing preparation or paperwork while class does something else
7. Arts and crafts, music
8. Exercises, physical and social games (nonacademic)
9. Intellectual games and contests
10. Nonacademic pastimes (reading to class, show and tell, puzzles and toys)
11. Unfocused small talk
12. Other (specify)

NOTES:

＃ 3, 5, 7 = *Reading Groups*
＃ 11, 13 = *Math lesson & seatwork*
＃ 9 = *outside recess (free play)*

CODES FOR EACH NEW ACTIVITY

	STARTING TIME	BEHAVIOR CODE	ELAPSED TIME
1.	8:15	1	15
2.	8:30	2	3
3.	8:33	4	27
4.	9:00	2	5
5.	9:05	4	25
6.	9:30	2	4
7.	9:34	4	36
8.	10:10	2	5
9.	10:15	8	15
10.	10:30	2	2
11.	10:32	3	38
12.	11:10	2	5
13.	11:15	5	30
14.	11:45	1	5
15.	11:50	Lunch	
16.			
17.			
18.			
19.			
20.			
21.			
22.			
23.			
24.			
25.			
26.			
27.			
28.			
29.			
30.			
31.			
32.			
33.			
34.			
35.			
36.			
37.			
38.			
39.			
40.			
41.			
42.			
43.			
44.			
45.			
36.			
47.			
48.			
49.			
50.			

TOTAL TIME PER CATEGORY

BEHAVIOR CODE	TOTAL MINUTES
1.	20
2.	24
3.	38
4.	88
5.	30
6.	
7.	
8.	15
9.	
10.	
11.	
12.	

Appendix 4: (*continued*)

This form describes how the teacher responds to students' questions.

FORM 5.2. Teacher's Response to Students' Questions

USE: When a student asks the teacher a reasonable question during a discussion or question-answer period
PURPOSE: To see if teacher models commitment to learning and concern for students' interests
Code each category that applies to the teacher's response to a reasonable student question. Do not code if student wasn't really asking a question or if he or she was baiting the teacher.

BEHAVIOR CATEGORIES	CODES	
1. Compliments the question ("Good question")	1. _4_	26. ___
2. Criticizes the question (unjustly) as irrelevant, dumb, out of place, etc.	2. _4_	27. ___
	3. _1,4_	28. ___
3. Ignores the question, or brushes it aside quickly without answering it	4. _4_	29. ___
	5. _4_	30. ___
4. Answers the question or redirects it to the class	6. _3_	31. ___
5. If no one can answer, teacher arranges to get the answer or assigns a student to do so	7. _4_	32. ___
	8. _4_	33. ___
6. If no one can answer, teacher leaves it un- answered and moves on	9. _7_	34. ___
7. Other (specify)	10. _4_	35. ___
	11. _4_	36. ___
NOTES:	12. ___	37. ___
	13. ___	38. ___
#7 *Explained that question would be covered in tomorrow's lesson.*	14. ___	39. ___
	15. ___	40. ___
	16. ___	41. ___
	17. ___	42. ___
	18. ___	43. ___
	19. ___	44. ___
	20. ___	45. ___
	21. ___	46. ___
	22. ___	47. ___
	23. ___	48. ___
	24. ___	49. ___
	25. ___	50. ___

---

8 Language and content: approaches to curriculum alignment

Jack C. Richards and Daniel Hurley

A major focus of language programs in many parts of the world is preparing students of limited proficiency in a second or foreign language to cope with school instruction in the new language. In many urban settings, there are large school-age populations of children with minimal or restricted proficiency in the school language. The options available at the school level vary according to school or district policy, school and teacher resources, and the age, background, and numbers of children involved. Students may receive an intensive language program before being mainstreamed, or they may enter classes that parallel regular classes in subjects such as science or social studies but are designed for students with limited proficiency in the school language.

In their mainstream classes, these students are expected to progress in school work at the same rate as other children of their age, despite not having a full command of the linguistic medium through which school subjects are being taught. In designing language programs that enable such students to make a successful transition to the mainstream classroom, many issues arise. What is the nature of the mainstream classroom? How can the second language curriculum support the mainstream curriculum? What demands does content learning place on students of limited proficiency in the school language? In this chapter the nature of these problems will be examined, drawing both on analytical reviews of research on classroom learning, as well as on observations of second language students in mainstream classroom settings.

Traditional approaches

Traditional approaches to instruction for students with limited proficiency in the school language focused almost exclusively on language proficiency. For example, the *New York State Core Curriculum for English as a Second Language in the Secondary Schools* (University of the State of New York 1983) sets out to specify the language skills needed for "limited English proficient students [to] attain communicative and linguistic competence." The curriculum lists goals for Listening, Speaking, Reading, Writing, and Culture across four levels of instruction, and specifies listening, speaking, reading and writing skills, grammatical structures, vocabulary, and cultural topics for each level.

The assumption underlying this kind of curriculum is that in order to succeed in the regular school system, the student needs further instruction in the school language. Cummins (1981: 4) characterizes this approach in these terms:

Lack of English proficiency is the major reason for language minority students' academic failure... When students have become proficient in English, then they can be exited to an all-English program, since limited English proficiency will no longer impede their academic progress.

In a language-based approach of this kind, learner needs are defined in terms of language skills, there is a primary focus on linguistic or communicative competence, language mastery is seen as the key to content learning and to academic achievement, and there is typically a separation of language learning from content learning (Mohan 1986). In recent years, however, there has been an increasing recognition that a language-skills approach reflects only part of the learner's total needs. Researchers and educators have stressed that if the goal of a second language program is to prepare students to participate in the regular school curriculum, it is necessary to examine more closely the relationship between language skill and academic achievement (Cummins 1981; Tikunoff 1985; Crandall 1987).

Limitations of traditional approaches

Cummins (1981) has explored the relationship between language proficiency and academic and cognitive development. The focus of Cummins's work has been on the nature of learning in school contexts. He observes that the skills needed for social interaction in the school are not necessarily the same as those needed for academic success. Cummins attributes this to differences in the cognitive demands of social-interactional and academic tasks. He distinguishes between two contexts for language use. Social-interactional uses of language, such as face-to-face conversation, are regarded as "context-embedded," since they are supported by the situation and by paralinguistic cues and allow for negotiation and feedback. Many academic tasks, however, such as reading or listening to a lecture, are regarded as "context-reduced," since the learner is forced to rely primarily on linguistic cues to meaning.

Cummins argues that academic success is dependent upon the ability to use language in context-reduced situations, whereas many second language programs focus primarily on using language in context-embedded settings. One consequence is that a learner may appear to be fluent

145

in the target language but may still have difficulty coping with the demands of the mainstream classroom. A common conclusion is that because the minority student is apparently fluent in the school language, poor academic performance cannot be attributed to language proficiency. Learning difficulties are consequently attributed to deficient cognitive abilities or to a lack of motivation.

The work of Brown et al. (1984) offers a complementary perspective on the nature of classroom discourse and the relationship between discourse management skills and classroom learning. They examined the oral language skills of native speakers of English in Scottish classrooms, and found that many native speakers lack the ability to use oral language effectively as a basis for classroom learning. Many students, while fluent in the interactional uses of language, lacked control of the discourse skills needed to communicate information effectively. They had difficulty performing tasks that required the coherent organization and presentation of specific information, tasks that the authors argue are basic to school achievement across the curriculum.

Saville-Troike (1984) examined how language proficiency and academic achievement are related. She found that ESL students' academic achievement in the content areas was not a factor of their English proficiency. Performance on language tests did not predict performance on content-based tests, nor did accuracy in English morphology and syntax affect academic performance. Among the conclusions she draws are:

1. Vocabulary knowledge in English is the most important aspect of oral English proficiency for academic achievement. Vocabulary taught in ESL should therefore be related as closely as possible to students' learning needs in their subject matter classes.
2. The portions of ESL lessons which focus on structural patterns, especially on English morphology, appear to make little contribution towards meeting students' immediate academic needs.

(Saville-Troike 1984: 216)

Saville-Troike concludes that second language programs have too often taught language as an end in itself rather than as a means to an end. They consequently fail to focus on the kinds of learning students encounter in regular classes. Mohan similarly observes that

any educational approach that considers language learning alone and ignores the learning of subject matter is inadequate to the needs of these learners ... What is needed is an integrative approach which relates language learning and content learning, considers language as a medium of learning, and acknowledges the role of context in communication. (1986: 1)

In order to develop such an approach, it is necessary to examine the nature of classroom learning and to consider the demands the main-

146

stream classroom creates for students of limited English proficiency. Many accounts have been given in recent years of the nature of classroom interaction and the processes that characterize classroom events (Barnes, Britton, and Rosen 1969; Doyle 1983; Cazden 1987; Chaudron 1988). Researchers from a variety of persuasions have examined classrooms in order to understand how learning is organized and accomplished. This research suggests that three crucial dimensions of classroom learning determine the success with which the student of limited second language proficiency can participate in the mainstream classroom.

First is the *interactional dimension*. This involves the ability to understand and use the social rules of classroom discourse in interacting with both peers and teachers. Successful class participation requires knowledge of rules and norms for initiating and maintaining communication with peers and teachers, and the skills needed to socialize in the classroom and school communities.

Second is the *instructional-task dimension*, which involves the ability to understand the nature of classroom learning and the manner in which classroom learning is accomplished. The primary focus is on the kinds of learning tasks that recur across subject areas in the school curriculum.

Last is the *cognitive dimension*, which involves the ability to understand and assimilate concepts, schemata, and information crucial to the content of different school subjects.

Tikunoff describes the ability to operate in these three dimensions of classroom behavior as constituting "student functional proficiency" (1985: 4). These dimensions of student functional proficiency will now be examined in more detail.

Interactional demands of the mainstream class

For children to be able to participate in a mainstream classroom, they need to possess the social skills that enable them to initiate contact both with their classmates and with the teacher, and to learn to manage such contact in appropriate ways. Wong Fillmore (1982) and Schinke-Llano (1983) found that when a mainstream class contains students with limited second language proficiency, the teacher tends to focus attention on the first language speakers in the classroom and to make relatively few demands on the others. In addition, the second language children tend to interact more frequently with other minority language children using their native tongue. They are not called on frequently to respond and so do not receive the same degree of input or feedback as the first language children. In addition, by not interacting with the other students in the class, the minority children are deprived of a major source of input for language development – the language of peers.

Another aspect of the interactional demands of the classroom concerns distinguishing between appropriate times for movement around the class and for individual seat work. Philips (1972) compared differences in classroom behavior between American Indian and non-Indian first graders. The Indian children failed to remain at their desks during seat work and instead wandered freely around the room. They spoke to other students while the teacher was talking and seemed more interested in interacting with their peers than with the teacher.

> In other words, there is, on the part of Indian students, relatively less interest, desire, and/or ability to internalize and act in accordance with some of the basic rules underlying classroom maintenance of orderly interaction. Most notably, Indian students are less willing than non-Indian students to accept the teacher as director and controller of all classroom activities. They are less interested in developing the one-to-one communicative relationship between teacher and student, and more interested in maintaining and developing relationships with their peers, regardless of what is going on in the classroom. (Philips 1972: 377)

Different perceptions of rules for turn-taking have also been observed. Both American Indians (Philips 1972) and native Hawaiians (Gallimore, Boggs, and Jordan 1974) have been found not to observe Anglo norms for bidding for turns. Children in both these groups tend to speak without raising their hand. At the same time, while Chinese or Filipino students may be comfortable giving silent attention to a dominant classroom authority figure, they may appear to lack initiative. In their own cultures, they are expected to wait to be called on, and to answer only when they are sure of being right (Cheng, n.d.; Teruya and Wong 1972). The experience of being singled out to respond individually may be uncomfortable for students of some cultural backgrounds for different reasons. Some children (such as Native Americans and Hawaiians) are more accustomed to functioning in a peer group, while others, such as Asians, may have learned to value humility and to avoid seeming to "show off." Similarly, nonverbal attention-getting strategies of Filipino and other students reveal a reluctance to call attention to oneself unnecessarily.

The child's understanding of what learning entails and how knowledge should be demonstrated presents another potential area of difficulty for minority students. For the American Indian children observed by Philips, learning consisted of observing adults silently and then imitating them, as opposed to verbally displaying knowledge in response to the teacher-centered questioning, which characterizes mainstream classrooms. This can lead to misinterpretation of minority student behaviors. Forman (1972) reports that a Filipino boy was judged by American teachers to be "hanging around," while Filipino teachers saw him as "listening attentively." In another case, a young Chicana was thought by her teacher to be unresponsive and a slow learner, until a videotape revealed that she spent much of her time interacting with other students and avoided direct interactions with the teacher (Carrasco 1981).

The demands of both individual and group work can also present difficulties for students from different backgrounds. Children from strong peer-group cultures may not initially perform well on individual tasks. Conversely, children accustomed to a highly competitive education system that values individual scholastic achievement may find it difficult to work cooperatively in groups.

Task demands of the mainstream class

The focus in this section is the nature of classroom work, the demands such work creates, and how such work is handled by children. What is it that children are required to do in order to participate effectively in classroom work, and how is the student of limited proficiency in the school language affected by the demands of class tasks?

Numerous attempts have been made to analyze the nature of classroom learning. Moore et al. (1986) isolate nine essential thinking processes that characterize classroom learning:

calling up	monitoring
connecting	reviewing
predicting	evaluating
organizing	applying
imaging	

These processes describe the role of the learner in bringing different informational schemata to bear on new material encountered in the classroom, through calling up prior knowledge and using it both to predict the new content of a lesson and to "connect" that content to more familiar information. Retention of the new material is aided by organizing it into a comprehensible framework, associating it with different images, monitoring for comprehension, and reviewing. Finally, the new knowledge is applied to different situations. Although proficiency in these different processes can facilitate learning, the familiarity of different learners with strategies for mastering them cannot be taken for granted. Less effective learners may, for example, approach each task or set of information either without relating it to an existing schemata or without recognizing when features of tasks or materials do not match those schemata. Similarly, a student may lack monitoring and reviewing strategies or may not perceive the applicability of different processes or information to new situations.

Doyle (1979, 1983) approaches the nature of classroom learning by describing the school curriculum as a collection of "tasks."

149

The term "task" focusses attention on three aspects of students' work: (a) the products students are to formulate, such as an original essay or answers to a set of test questions; (b) the operations that are to be used to generate the product, such as memorizing a list of words or classifying examples of a concept; and (c) the "givens" or resources available to students while they are generating a product, such as a model of a finished essay supplied by the teacher or a fellow student. Academic tasks, in other words, are defined by the answers students are required to produce and the routes that can be used to obtain these answers. (1983: 162)

Doyle points out that the typical labels used to describe classroom tasks are not informative. What is meant by "writing" in one class may refer to students copying a model composition from the board and making minor additions to it, whereas in another it may refer to a process by which students choose a topic to write about, generate ideas about it, and then go through a cycle of drafting and revising to produce a final product. Doyle suggests that school work is defined by a core of basic tasks that recur across different subjects in the curriculum. Tasks hence define the nature of learning in classrooms as well as the conditions for its success. They determine how information is to be processed, how learning will occur, and how the results of learning will be demonstrated.
    Doyle (1983) identifies four tasks as central to all classroom work:

1. memory tasks, which require students to reproduce previously presented information
2. procedural or routine tasks, in which students are expected to apply fixed routines or procedures in order to generate answers
3. comprehension or understanding tasks, in which students are required to make inferences, recognize new versions of information previously encountered, and solve problems
4. opinion tasks, in which students are expected to state a preference for something.

Task, in Doyle's sense, exists at the macro level of classroom processes and refers to learning activities that are common to different subject areas. At the micro level, however, as will be illustrated, there may be significant differences within subjects, reflecting the cognitive processes, content, and knowledge schemata of particular subjects in the school curriculum.
    Tikunoff (1985: 19–21) suggests that in order to complete classroom tasks effectively, a student needs to

1. understand the expectations of different kinds of classroom tasks, knowing what the intended product or outcome of a class task should be when it is completed, and how to complete it
2. participate productively in classroom tasks, maintaining active en-

gagement in tasks, completing tasks accurately, and observing the teacher's norms for class tasks

3. obtain feedback on tasks, knowing how to obtain feedback, whether from the teacher or someone else in the classroom who possesses appropriate information.

In addition, Tikunoff suggests, students must understand the instructional demands of classroom tasks and activities in terms of

order – knowing the order in which tasks will be completed

pacing – knowing the optimal amount of time that can be spent on a task and the time by when it should be completed

product – knowing the kind of product (e.g., book report, workbook entry) expected for specific kinds of tasks

learning strategies – choosing appropriate learning strategies for tasks

participation – knowing if the task should be completed individually or in cooperation with others

resources – knowing what resources and materials to use with different tasks.

The demands of classroom tasks pose many kinds of problems for the minority child. In the area of participation, for example, it was noted earlier that students may not recognize the different task demands of silent individual work (in tests or seat work) or group work (problem solving), depending on the degree of peer-group orientation or academic competitiveness fostered by school experiences in their native cultures. They may also be unfamiliar with the learning strategies required in a task or the teacher's expectations for that task – its "product," as illustrated in this interaction in a math class, cited by Dale and Cuevas (1987: 9–10).

The teacher has written this equation on the board: $(6 + 5) + 4 \square 6 + (5 + 4)$

Teacher: Are they equal?
Student (English proficient): Yes, they are.
Teacher: (*pointing to an LEP student*) How do you know?
LEP Student: They equal.
Teacher: Yes, we know. But, tell me, why are they equal?
LEP Student: It is equal.
Teacher: O.K. They are equal because both number sentences have the same sum. Now, what symbol can we write in the empty square?
Native English-Speaking Student: Equal sign!
Teacher: Right! Very good! (*now pointing to an LEP student*) Please write the equal sign inside the square.
LEP Student: (*Obviously not quite sure of what it is she is supposed to do, she goes to the board and writes the answer to each number sentence.*)

151

Teacher: Good! Tell me what symbol do we write in the *square* to say that
   this side (*pointing*) is *equal* to this side?
LEP Student: (*Appears embarrassed, lowers her head and does not answer*).

As Dale and Cuevas point out, the child's difficulties here are caused
partly by a lack of linguistic resources. However, when the teacher "steps
back" from a more or less routine task at hand (in this case, solving
equations) to probe higher levels of analysis, more than linguistic resources are needed. Familiarity with the learning strategies and thought
processes involved in discussing math is required, as well as knowledge
that these kinds of processes are an expected component of the task.

Cognitive demands of the mainstream class

In addition to the general task demands of classroom learning, it is also
necessary to consider the particular demands of learning academically
demanding school content, such as math, science, or social studies,
through a second language. These can be called the "cognitive" demands
of the curriculum.

There are three major dimensions to the cognitive demands of content-
related instruction:

1. the ability to assimilate new concepts and information associated
   with specific subject areas in the curriculum
2. the ability to use and understand the linguistic resources employed
   within particular content domains
3. the ability to use and understand particular modes of inquiry associated with specific content domains.

The need to understand new concepts is crucial in a subject such as
social studies, in which concepts such as "conflict," "liberty," "equal
opportunity," "minority rights," and "prejudice" might be crucial to a
lesson on the rights of blacks. A child entering a fifth grade social studies
class is assumed to be familiar with background concepts and schemata
acquired in earlier grades. Without a full understanding of many of these
concepts, the child will not be able to understand the content of the fifth
grade social studies curriculum.

Social studies also presents a particular set of linguistic challenges to
the LEP student. Chamot and O'Malley (1986) cite the State of Mary-
land's requirement that 94 vocabulary items be learned in preparation
for a citizenship competency exam. They also illustrate the difficult mix
of vocabulary and concepts peculiar to social studies in the following
example, taken from a study guide for high school social studies:

Federalism means the division of governmental powers between the national
and state governments. Both levels of government may act directly on citizens

through their own officials and laws. Both levels of government derive their power to act from our Constitution. Each level of government has certain subjects over which its powers are supreme. Both levels of government must agree to changes in the Constitution. (p. 68)

Social studies texts tend to have particular patterns of discourse, in which a passage listing a series of facts and dates is followed by one where this information is explained. At the level of sentence structure, students must also be able to decode cause-and-effect structures, and where historical events or trends are discussed, negotiate a complex mix of verb tenses. In addition, a greater degree of inferencing and evaluation may be called for in social studies than in other areas of the curriculum.

In math, different kinds of problems exist. The vocabulary contains many words unique to math (e.g., *divisor* or *coefficient*), has equivalent forms of different concepts that must be recognized (e.g., "subtract from," "decrease by," "less," "minus," and "take away" all represent subtraction), and has words that have meanings in math texts different from their usage elsewhere (e.g., *rational* and *table*). At the level of syntax, the standard word order of English sentences must often be reversed in writing math problems:

"eight divided by two" is written mathematically as $2\,\overline{)\,8.}$

Additionally, at the discourse level, math problems often possess a certain ambiguity stemming from the relative lack of redundancy in the discourse of math, as compared to ordinary prose:

Food expenses take 25% of the average family's income. A family makes $700 a month. How much is spent on food?

Students who can solve this problem generally are not bothered by the fact that the problem does not specify directly the amount that is being asked for, that is, the amount per month? the amount per year? ... Students who are not proficient in the language of word problems would demand a paraphrase or repetition of the time reference to clarify the problem question. (Dale and Cuevas 1987: 23)

In the sciences, knowledge of particular schemata is needed to participate in different kinds of scientific discourse. Dansereau (1985) provides an example of a schema that is needed to study scientific theories:

1. *Description* A short summary of the theory which includes
   a. Phenomena
   b. Predictions
   c. Observations
   d. Definitions
2. *Inventor/History* A brief account of the theory's history, which includes
   a. Name(s)

153

   b. Date
   c. Historical background
3. *Consequences*   A concise summary of how the theory has influenced man. This includes
   a. Applications
   b. Beliefs
4. *Evidence*   A short summary of facts that support or refute the theory. This includes
   a. Experiments
   b. Observations
5. *Other Theories*   A concise summary of theories dealing with the same phenomena. These are usually of two types:
   a. Competing theories
   b. Similar theories

In the area of language, the vocabulary of science poses considerable demands on the minority student. Hurd et al. (1981) report that intermediate science texts introduce an average of 2,500 new terms in each year of instruction. In addition, scientific discourse uses different syntactic devices to signal that different processes are involved or that different types of information are being presented. For example, hypotheses are likely to contain a number of if–then sentences and use the conditional (Mohan 1986). At the discourse level, learners must be able to distinguish between statements of fact (e.g., descriptions of effects) and statements that are not factual (e.g., hypotheses, inferences). The learner must also be able to organize and interpret experiments and information, making productive use of these different schemata.

Implications for program design

The preceding discussion has suggested that effective participation in the mainstream classroom has three interrelated dimensions, referred to here as the interactional dimension, the instructional-task dimension, and the cognitive dimension. An effective language program for students of limited proficiency in the school language must address each of these dimensions of student functional proficiency if it is to give minority students an adequate preparation for the demands of the mainstream classroom. This is the issue of curriculum alignment, that is, ensuring that the second language curriculum reflects the content and processes of the regular school curriculum. At the same time, the second language program can only partially prepare students for regular classroom instruction. The mainstream teacher also shares the responsibility for ensuring that he or she teaches to all of the students in the class and not just majority students. (Procedures that teachers can use in monitoring these and other aspects of their teaching are discussed in Chapter 7.) What instructional options are available to address these problems?

With regard to the interactional dimension, one option is for the teacher to modify the interactional structure of the classroom in order to assist the minority child in acquiring appropriate classroom interactional skills. A strategy available to teachers who speak the students' home language is to use the children's home language to mediate effective instruction. In a study of successful bilingual education teachers, teachers were observed to make frequent use of their minority students' home language and culture in order to promote classroom participation and interaction:

> Teacher's use of cultural information took linguistic as well as non-verbal form in three ways: (1) responding to or using L1 cultural referents to enhance instruction, (2) organizing instructional activities to build upon ways in which limited English proficient students naturally participate in discourse in their own home cultures, and (3) recognizing and honoring the values and norms of the students' home cultures while teaching those of the majority culture. (Tikunoff 1985: 92)

Cazden et al. (1980) cite further examples of teachers' successfully bridging the cultural gap between the home and school cultures. A Hispanic first grade teacher created some home–school continuity by reinforcing values taught at home, demonstrating familiarity with the family and community lives of her students, and employing first language communicative strategies (in this case, the use of diminutives) to create a comfortable atmosphere in the classroom. Similarly, a Filipina teacher observed by Ongteco (1987) used both linguistic and cultural strategies to put her students at ease. At the same time, her patterns of questions, nominations, and other components of classroom discourse management shifted over a semester from a highly teacher-centered pattern of controlled nominations focused on discrete answers (a "product" focus) to one more closely resembling the open bidding pattern observed in a mainstream classroom in the same school (i.e., a "process" focus). In this way, while making the course content and interactional patterns manageable for her students at the beginning of the term, she acquainted them gradually with the interactive and cognitive tasks needed for entry into the mainstream classroom.

With regard to the instructional-task dimension, observation of effective content teachers suggests that they monitor their own teaching and their students' performance to ensure that students understand the demands of different kinds of classroom tasks, and participate appropriately and effectively in classroom tasks. Table 8.1 shows the relationship between teacher behavior and student performance on tasks.

Chamot and O'Malley (1986) discuss an approach to program design

TABLE 8.1. RELATIONSHIPS OF CHARACTERISTICS OF A FUNCTIONALLY
PROFICIENT STUDENT WITH ACTIVE TEACHING

So that students can:	*Teachers must:*
Decode, understand: Task expectations (what product should look like; how to complete accurately) New information	*Communicate clearly:* Give accurate directions Specify tasks and measurements Present new information by explaining, outlining, summarizing, reviewing
Participate productively: Maintain productive engagement on assigned tasks and complete them Complete tasks with high accuracy Know when successful in tasks Observe norms (meet teacher's expectations)	*Obtain, maintain engagement:* Maintain task focus Pace instruction appropriately Promote involvement Communicate expectations for successful performance
Obtain feedback: Know how to obtain accurate feedback re: task completion, i.e., whether achieving accuracy or how to achieve accuracy	*Monitor progress...* Review work frequently Adjust instruction to maximize accuracy *...and provide immediate feedback:* Re: task completion so students know when they are successful or are given information about how to achieve success

Source: Tikunoff (1985: 32).

that attempts to address the interactional, instructional-task, and cognitive dimensions of mainstream content instruction by focusing on three kinds of learner strategies:

Metacognitive strategies, which involve executive processes for learning, monitoring one's comprehension and production, and evaluating how well one has achieved a learning objective;

Cognitive strategies, in which the learner interacts with the material to be learned by manipulating it mentally (as in making mental images or transferring previously acquired concepts or skills), or physically (as in grouping items to be learned in meaningful categories or taking notes on important information to be remembered);

Social-affective strategies, in which the learner either interacts with another person in order to assist learning, as in cooperation or asking questions for clarification, or uses some kind of affective control to assist a learning task.

(Chamot and O'Malley 1986: 17)

In addition, the language development component of the program focuses on

Development of the specialized vocabulary and technical terms of each content area;
Practice with the language functions used in academic communication, such as explaining, informing, describing, classifying and evaluating;
Development of the ability to comprehend and use the language structures and discourse features found in different subject areas; and
Practice in using the language skills needed in the content classroom, such as listening to explanations, reading for information, participating in academic discussions, and writing reports.

(p. 15)

Chamot and O'Malley illustrate how these principles can be applied to the development of lessons in science, math, and social studies, thus providing a transitional level before entering the mainstream academic curriculum (see Appendix).

A program with similar goals is described by King et al. (1987). They describe a content-based program that seeks to develop students' knowledge of vocabulary and concepts as well as to develop the study skills and critical thinking skills needed for success in mainstream content classes. Practical suggestions for ways of achieving curriculum alignment through the integration of language development with content instruction are also given in Mohan (1986), Cantoni-Harvey (1987), and Crandall (1987), although these texts discuss primarily the third dimension of student functional proficiency – the cognitive dimension – and have little to say about the interactional or instructional-task dimensions. Another issue less frequently discussed in the literature on content-based instruction is the influence of external factors. In the United States, for example, local programs for minority students must meet federal guidelines that gauge the success of a second language program by the rapidity with which students are mainstreamed, based on performance on a standardized language proficiency test. Such a requirement will obviously have a major influence on the design of a second language program.

Conclusions

Program planners, textbook writers, and language teachers now have a variety of options to choose from in developing content-based approaches to second language instruction. The present analysis has suggested that the basis for appropriate instructional designs is the notion of student functional proficiency and its interactional, task, and cognitive components. Approaches that address only the linguistic dimensions of

157

the problem ignore the complexity of classroom learning and classroom interaction through the medium of a second or foreign language. At the same time, a broader research base is essential to provide information for program planning and evaluation. This would provide three kinds of data:

1. Information on how successful second language programs for students with limited proficiency in the school language integrate second language development with content-focused instruction. Case studies and observational accounts of successful programs could provide this kind of information.
2. Information on what it is that effective minority students do to cope with the demands of mainstream classes. Observational data and research on learner strategies could provide information in this category.
3. Information on what it is that effective mainstream teachers do to accommodate their instructional style to students with limited proficiency in the school language.

This information will allow for a more successful alignment of the second language and mainstream curriculums, enabling minority students to participate more fully in the mainstream classroom.

Discussion topics and activities

1. Observe a content class (e.g., at a school, college, or university). Can you identify behaviors, processes, activities, or content that relate to
   a) the interactional dimension of classrooms?
   b) the instructional-task dimension?
   c) the cognitive dimension?
2. Can you suggest examples of how students from different cultural groups have different expectations concerning the interactional demands of the classroom?
3. Discuss examples of the four kinds of tasks discussed by Doyle (p. 150) as they relate to specific subjects in the school curriculum.
4. Examine a lesson or chapter from an elementary or high school content textbook (e.g., social studies, geography). Look at Tikunoff's list of the instructional demands of learning in terms of order, pacing, product, learning strategies, participation, and resources (pp. 150–151), and analyze the lesson according to these dimensions.
5. Examine a content textbook and try to find examples of the three cognitive dimensions discussed on page 152 (concepts, linguistic

resources, modes of inquiry) that might pose particular problems for students with limited English proficiency.

6. Examine a content textbook and try to identify a schema associated with a particular topic or subject area (e.g., such as that for scientific theory discussed on pp. 153–154).

7. Prepare a lesson plan that addresses student functional proficiency (p. 147) – that is, that integrates language learning and content learning.

Appendix: Sample lesson plan

This lesson plan addresses both language proficiency and the instructional-task and cognitive dimensions of a content subject (Science).

Sample Science Lesson 1: Rocks and Water

Language Objectives:	Oral language development, listening comprehension, note-taking, report writing
Science Objectives:	Find out the effects of moving water on rocks, find out the effects of rocks on water, develop the concept of a fair sample, practice observation and recording skills
Learning Strategies:	Metacognitive – selective attention, self-evaluation. Cognitive – transfer, inferencing, imagery, note-taking. Social-affective – cooperation, questions for clarification
Grade Level:	Upper elementary
Materials for Each Group:	One paper or plastic bag; three jars of the same size, with lids; three paper towels; approximately thirty small, sharp stones or about 18–24 sharp fragments broken from a brick (some groups can have stones and others brick fragments); two tall glasses; water. For each student: a small notebook as an observation journal.

PREPARATION

1. Discuss with students what happens to rain water. When it rains, where does the water go? Elicit that water runs downhill to form streams and rivers, and that these bodies of running water flow downhill into other rivers, lakes, or oceans. Write any new vocabulary on the board as it is discussed.
2. Ask students to speculate what happens as water moves over the land. What happens to the land? What happens to the water? Write student contributions on the board. Some students' predictions may be based on previous knowledge, and others may be hypotheses. The experimental activities that follow will serve both to illustrate previous knowledge and to test hypotheses.

PRESENTATION

1. Explain to students that they will be working in groups to find out what water does to rocks and what rocks do to water.

Reprinted with permission from A. U. Chamot and J. M. O'Malley, *A Cognitive Academic Language Learning Approach: An ESL Content-Based Curriculum*. Rosslyn, Va.: National Clearinghouse for Bilingual Education, 1986. This lesson was adapted from *Addison-Wesley Science*, Book 4, © 1980 by Addison-Wesley, Reading, Mass.

2. Ask students to take notes on the following information and directions for the experiment. Remind students to use abbreviations, key words, and phrases rather than sentences, and diagrams or drawings to clarify meanings.

When water flows over land in streams and rivers, it moves pieces of rock. When rock pieces move, they hit each other and they hit the bottom of the stream. Small bits of the rock pieces break off. The rock pieces become more rounded and less sharp. Small bits of rock dissolve in the water of the stream. To find out what water does to rocks and what rocks do to water, we are going to do an experiment. These are the steps:

   1. Make three piles of stones, equal in number. Each pile should have the same kinds of stones.
   2. Put each pile of stones in a jar. Label the jars A, B, and C.
   3. Fill Jars A and B half full of water. Put the lids on all three jars and close them tightly.
   4. Put Jar A in a bag (to protect it in case it breaks).
   5. Shake Jar A 1000 times. Do not shake Jars B and C.
   6. Label the two glasses A and B.
   7. Pour the water from Jar A into Glass A. Pour the water from Jar B into Glass B.
   8. Label three paper towels A, B, and C.
   9. Pour the stones from Jar A onto Paper Towel A, from Jar B onto Paper Towel B, and from Jar C onto Paper Towel C.
   10. Observe the water in Glass A and Glass B. Write down your observations.
   11. Observe the stones on the three towels. Write down your observations.

3. Explain to students what a fair sample is. (A fair sample is a random selection of items.) Ask them to think of ways to make sure that the three piles of stones are alike in range of stone sizes, shapes, and colors. (Suggested method: Have students pick stones with eyes closed to ensure random selection.)
4. Provide students with format for observation journal. The format can be similar to the following, depending on the grade level:

Name
Date
Name of Experiment
Prediction (What I think will happen)
Procedures (What we did)
Results (what happened to the water; what happened to the stones)

If the follow-up activities are carried out, the "Procedures" and "Results" sections of the report should be repeated and dated as necessary.

PRACTICE

1. Divide students into small groups. Each group should compare the notes they have taken on the steps for the experiment, and ask questions for

clarification for any steps that they do not understand or did not write down clearly. Have the groups prepare a master procedure card with all the steps for the experiment, and diagrams as needed.

2. When each group has a clear understanding of the steps to follow, have them decide which students will undertake each step, and write their names next to that step on the master procedure card. Students should take turns shaking Jar A, and should decide on how many shakes each should make, recording them as completed.

3. Provide each group with the materials listed above and have students carry out the experiment. Save the water in the glasses and the stones in the three piles for the follow-up activities.

4. Have students record the experiment in their individual observation journals (see #4 under "Presentation"). The expected results of this experiment are: the water in Glass A will be more clouded than the water in Glass B because of stone fragments dissolved in it through the action of 1000 shakes; the piles of stones on Paper Towel A will be more rounded (less sharp) than the other 2 piles of stones.

EVALUATION

1. Have students share their observation journals with one or more classmates who worked with another group on the experiment to compare and discuss their entries.

2. Provide students with four to five stones or rocks of different shapes. Ask them to classify them according to how much contact with water they have probably had. (Smooth, rounded stones probably have had most contact; sharp, jagged stones the least. However, the hardness of the rock is also a factor – harder rocks are more resistant to the wearing effects of water.)

FOLLOW-UP

1. Have students replace the stones and water into their original jars and continue to shake Jar A 1000 times a day, recording predictions and results in their observation journals.

2. Have students bring in small samples of water from different sources such as: homes, lakes, mud puddles, water fountain, Jars A and B, fresh rain water, etc. Have them mark glass slides to identify the source of the water, and then put several drops of water on each slide. After the water has dried, have them compare and discuss the sediment remaining. (The more transparent the residue, the less rock/minerals dissolved in the water.) Discuss the differences between hard and soft water.

3. Have students do research and keep observation journals about the effects of water on land. A field trip to a stream before and after a rainstorm can provide a first-hand experience with the effects of water on land. Students can share their journals and reports in small groups or with the whole class.

Conclusion: a look toward the future

The aim of this book has been to examine the language teaching matrix – that is, the interactions between teachers, learners, the curriculum, classroom activities, and instructional materials – and to try to account for how different aspects of this process can be described, planned, implemented, and monitored. In doing so, I looked at some of the key issues that shape the field of second and foreign language teaching. Language teaching, somewhat more than other areas of educational focus, has been subject to constant changing enthusiasm for different "solutions" to the language teaching challenge. Typically, however, innovators focus on a single dimension of what is inevitably a multi-dimensional phenomenon. As Clark (1985: 6) puts it:

Much unnecessary confusion has been created by those who have thought the solution to the language curriculum problem could be found in one part of the jigsaw to the exclusion of other parts. Thus, panaceas have been sought in methodology alone, or in catch-all technological aids ... or in 'graded tests', as if assessment by itself could improve the teaching/learning process, or in the elaboration of ever more complex syllabuses such as the various Threshold documents, or in studies of second language acquisition, or the impressionistic global descriptions of proficiency at different levels.

My own view is likewise that the field of second and foreign language teaching requires a comprehensive view of how successful learning and teaching is planned for and accomplished in educational settings. This perspective involves approaching language teaching as a particular case of educational program design. It has far more in common with the field of curriculum development than with linguistics. From a curriculum development perspective, each of the elements in the language teaching matrix is necessarily involved in any kind of educational program design.

Some issues will center on questions of content and the kinds of knowledge and skills (e.g., in reading, writing, listening, or speaking) the program is expected to address. Relevant questions to be addressed in the process of educational design will include:

What is the nature of the "knowledge" the program is expected to teach? Is it well-defined and understood by both teachers and learners?
How can this view of knowledge or content be reflected in instructional approaches and in instructional materials?

163

Is the process of acquiring this knowledge or content believed to be a long-term, mid-term or short-term process?

Another important set of questions will seek to develop a profile of the instructional factors that will affect the design and delivery of instruction. Here the input of teachers, paraprofessionals, resource people, content specialists, and other staff involved in the program is needed. Information will be required on planned or preferred instructional strategies and tactics, programs and materials, technologies, educational environments, time and scheduling, and techniques and plans for reporting on learner progress to the learners themselves, to teachers, to administrators, and to other interested parties. Relevant questions will include:

Is there an instructional program that learners and teachers are expected to follow?
Are instructional goals and strategies well defined and agreed upon?
How do teachers view their role in the instructional process?
How is effective teaching in the program defined?
How is instruction monitored and evaluated?
What background experience and training do teachers have and what are the possibilities for teacher renewal?
What kind of communication, cooperation, and coordination exists or is possible between teachers within an instructional unit?

Information on the learners in the program is also crucial. The learner domain involves issues relating to the ages, proficiency levels, and developmental stages of the learners. It includes as well social background characteristics, worldviews, and learning expectations. Considerations include students' self-perceptions and prior learning experiences as well as preferred learning styles, strategies, environments, and groupings. The student domain involves responses to such questions as:

How are the learners characterized, by themselves and others?
Who determines learning goals for students and how are these goals communicated to students?
Can learning styles and strategies be determined?
What mechanisms exist for learner input into the program?
How are students selected, assigned, evaluated, and "graduated"?

Last, the nature of the administrative context that supports and monitors the program must be determined. In studies of programmatic educational change, three administrative influences are typically identified – those from the central office, those from the "program," and those from the schools. Administrative considerations at all these levels will determine the scale, pace, and style of educational delivery. The administrative domain involves answers to such questions as:

Are the critical administrative groups clearly identified?

Are they personally and professionally compatible?

Are communication channels to, from, and between administrators and teachers clearly defined and open?

How are administrative latitude, pressure, and/or support perceived by teachers?

What sort of commitment do administrative agents have to the program?

Central to this process, however, is the role of the teacher. One of the consequences of the curriculum-based view of language teaching proposed here is a redefinition of the role of the teacher. No longer simply a presenter of materials or an implementer of a method, the teacher now has a role that is not only more complex but more crucial, for the teacher must serve variously as materials developer, needs analyst, and investigator of his or her own classroom, negotiating both syllabus content and methodology with the learner. Rather than methods determining the curriculum, the school and the classroom are seen as the context in which planning, development, and support activities take place. A number of implications for teacher education and teacher development follow from this redefinition of the teacher's role.

1. Teacher preparation programs must move beyond a "training" perspective to an "education" perspective – one which recognizes that successful teaching involves higher-level cognitive processes that cannot be taught directly.
2. Teachers and student teachers need to adopt a research orientation to their own classrooms and their own teaching.
3. Language programs should reflect less of an emphasis on prescriptions and top-down directives and more of an emphasis on inquiry-based and discovery-oriented approaches to learning and teaching – a more bottom-up perspective.
4. Teacher preparation programs should include experiences that require student teachers to generate theories and hypotheses, and to reflect critically on teaching through gathering data about teaching and learning.
5. There will inevitably be less dependence on linguistics and language theory as a source discipline for teaching and teacher education and more of an attempt to integrate sound, educationally based approaches.

References

Allen, P., M. Fröhlich, and N. Spada. 1985. The communicative orientation of language teaching: an observation scheme. *Foreign Language Annals* 18: 25–9.

Armstrong, S., and G. Frith. 1984. *Practical Self-Monitoring for Classroom Use.* Springfield, Ill.: Charles Thomas.

Ashton-Warner, S. 1965. *Teacher.* New York: Simon & Schuster.

Bachman, L. F. 1981. Formative evaluation in specific purpose program development. In R. Mackay and J. Palmer (eds.), *Language for Specific Purposes*, pp. 106–116. Rowley, Mass.: Newbury House.

Bailey, K. M. 1983. Competitiveness and anxiety in adult second language learning: looking at and through the diary studies. In Seliger and Long (eds.), 1983.

1990. The use of diary studies in teacher education programs. In J. C. Richards and D. Nunan (eds.), *Second Language Teacher Education.* New York: Cambridge University Press.

Barnes, D., J. Britton, and H. Rosen. 1969. *Language, the Learner and School.* Baltimore: Penguin.

Berliner, D. C. 1984. The half-full glass: a review of research on teaching. In P. L. Hosford (ed.), *Using What We Know about Teaching*, pp. 51–77. Alexandria, Va.: Association for Supervision and Curriculum Development.

Blum, R. E. 1984. *Effective Schooling Practices: A Research Synthesis.* Portland, Ore.: Northwest Regional Educational Laboratory.

Blundell, L., and J. Stokes. 1981. *Task Listening.* Cambridge: Cambridge University Press.

Bode, S., and S. Lee. 1987. *Overheard and Understood.* Belmont, Cal.: Wadsworth.

Bright, J. A., and G. P. McGregor. 1970. *Teaching English as a Second Language.* London: Longman.

Brindley, G. 1984. *Needs Analysis and Objective Setting in the Australian Migrant Education Program.* Sydney: NSW Migrant Education Service.

Brown, G., A. Anderson, R. Shilcock, and G. Yule. 1984. *Teaching Talk: Strategies for Production and Assessment.* Cambridge: Cambridge University Press.

Brown, G., and G. Yule, 1983. *Teaching the Spoken Language.* Cambridge: Cambridge University Press.

Brown, P., and S. Levinson. 1978. Universals in language use: politeness phenomena. In E. N. Goody (ed.), *Questions and Politeness: Strategies in Social Interaction.* Cambridge: Cambridge University Press.

Bygate, M. 1987. *Speaking.* Oxford: Oxford University Press.

167

References

Canale, M. 1982. Evaluating the coherence of student writing in L1 and L2. Paper presented at the annual TESOL Convention, Honolulu, Hawaii.

Cantoni-Harvey, G. 1987. *Content-Area Language Instruction: Approaches and Strategies*. Reading, Mass.: Addison-Wesley.

Carey, J. 1986. Not-teaching writing: discovering the writing process. *Carleton Papers in Applied Language Studies 111: 47–76*.

Carrasco, R. L. 1981. Expanded awareness of student performance: a case study in applied ethnographic monitoring in a bilingual classroom. In H. Trueba, G. P. Guthrie, and K. H. Au (eds.), *Culture and the Bilingual Classroom: Studies in Classroom Ethnography*. Rowley, Mass.: Newbury House.

Carrell, P., J. Devine, and D. Eskey (eds.). 1988. *Interactive Approaches to Second Language Reading*. New York: Cambridge University Press.

Cazden, C. 1987. Classroom discourse. In M. C. Wittrock (ed.), *Handbook of Research on Teaching*. New York: Macmillan.

Cazden, C., R. Carrasco, A. A. Maldonado-Guzman, and F. Erickson. 1980. The contribution of ethnographic research to bilingual education. In J. E. Alatis (ed.), *Current Issues in Bilingual Education*, pp. 64–80. Georgetown University Round Table on Languages and Linguistics. Washington, D. C.: Georgetown University Press.

Chall, J. 1967. *Learning to Read: The Great Debate*. New York: McGraw-Hill.

Chamot, A. U., and J. M. O'Malley. 1986. *A Cognitive Academic Language Learning Approach: An ESL Content-Based Curriculum*. Rosslyn, Va.: National Clearinghouse for Bilingual Education.

Chaudron, C. 1988. *Second Language Classrooms: Research on Teaching and Learning*. New York: Cambridge University Press.

Chaudron, C., and J. C. Richards. 1986. The effect of discourse markers on the comprehension of lectures. *Applied Linguistics 7*, 2: 113–27.

Cheng, L. No date. Cultural perspectives: contrastive cultural analysis. Unpublished report. Department of Communication Disorders, San Diego State University.

Christison, M. A., and S. Bassano. 1984. Teacher self-observation. *TESOL Newsletter 18*, 4: 17–19.

Clark, H. M., and E. V. Clark. 1977. *Psychology and Language: An Introduction to Psycholinguistics*. New York: Harcourt Brace Jovanovich.

Clark, J. 1985. Curriculum renewal. Keynote address to the Australian Association of Applied Linguistics, Brisbane, August.

Cohen, A. D., and E. Aphek. 1980. Retention of second-language vocabulary over time: investigating the role of mnemonic associations. *System 8:* 221–35.

Coulthard, M. 1977. *Discourse Analysis*. London: Longman.

Crandall, J. (ed.). 1987. *ESL through Content-Area Instruction: Mathematics, Science, Social Studies*. Englewood Cliffs, N.J.: Prentice-Hall.

Cummins, J. 1981. The role of primary language development in promoting educational success for language minority children. In *Schooling and Language Minority Students: A Theoretical Framework*, pp. 3–49. Los Angeles: National Evaluation, Dissemination, and Assessment Center, California State University.

Dale, T. C., and G. J. Cuevas. 1987. Integrating language and mathematics learning. In Crandall (ed.), pp. 9–54.

Dansereau, D. F. 1985. Learning strategy research. In J. W. Segal, S. F. Chapman, and R. Glaser (eds.), *Thinking and Learning Skills*, pp. 209–49. Hillsdale, N.J.: Erlbaum.

Davies, A., and H. G. Widdowson. 1974. Reading and writing. In J. P. B. Allen and S. P. Corder (eds.), *The Edinburgh Course in Applied Linguistics*, Vol. 3. London: Oxford University Press.

Dick, W., and L. Carey. 1985. *The Systematic Design of Instruction*. Glenview, Ill.: Scott Foresman.

Doyle, W. 1977. Paradigms for research on teacher effectiveness. In L. S. Shulman (ed.), *Review of Research in Teacher Education*, Vol. 5, pp. 163–98. Itasca, Ill.: Peacock.

1979. Classroom tasks and students' abilities. In P. L. Peterson and H. J. Walberg (eds.), *Research on Teaching: Concepts, Findings and Implications*, pp. 183–209. Berkeley: McCutchan.

1983. Academic work. *Review of Educational Research 53*, 2: 159–99.

Dunkin, M., and B. Biddle. 1974. *The Study of Teaching*. New York: Holt, Rinehart and Winston.

Elliot, J. 1980. Implications of classroom research for professional development. In E. Hoyle and J. Megarry (eds.), *World Yearbook of Education, 1980*, pp. 308–24. London: Kogan Page.

Emig, J. 1971. *The Composing Processes of 12th Graders*. Champaign, Ill.: National Council of Teachers of English.

English Language Syllabus in Malaysian Schools. 1975. Kuala Lumpur: Dewan Bahasa Dan Pustaka.

Eschholz, P. A. 1980. The prose models approach: using products in the process. In T. R. Donovan and W. McClelland (eds.), *Eight Approaches to the Teaching of Composition*, pp. 21–36. Urbana, Ill.: National Council of Teachers of English.

Evertson, C. M., L. M. Anderson, and J. E. Brophy. 1978. The Texas junior high school study: report of process-product relationships. University of Texas, Research and Development Center for Teacher Education, Austin.

Fanselow, J. F. 1977. Beyond "Rashomon": conceptualizing and describing the teaching act. *TESOL Quarterly 11*, 1: 17–39.

Fassman, P., and S. Tavares. 1985. *Fast Forward*. New York: Longman.

Fillmore, C. J. 1979. On fluency. In C. Fillmore (ed.), *Individual Differences in Language Ability and Language Behavior*. New York: Academic Press.

Findlay, C. A., and L. A. Nathan. 1980. Functional language objectives in a competency based ESL curriculum. *TESOL Quarterly 14*, 2: 221–33.

Fisher, C. W., D. C. Berliner, N. N. Filby, R. S. Marliave, L. S. Cahen, and M. M. Dishaw. 1980. Teaching behaviors, academic learning time and academic achievement: an overview. In C. Denham and A. Lieberman (eds.), *Time to Learn*, pp. 7–32. Washington, D.C.: U.S. Department of Education, National Institute of Education.

Flower, L. 1979. Writer-based prose: a cognitive basis for problems in writing. *College English 41*: 19–37.

169

References

Flower, L., and J. Hayes. 1980. The cognition of discovery: defining a rhetorical problem. *College Composition and Communication 31:* 21–32.

1981. A cognitive process theory of writing. *College Composition and Communication 32:* 365–87.

Forman, S. 1972. Cultural differences in response to filmed child sequences. Master's thesis. University of Hawaii at Manoa.

Fraser, H., and A. Skibicki. 1987. Self-directed learning strategies for adult Vietnamese learners of ESL. *Prospect 3,* 1: 33–44.

Gallimore, R., J. Boggs, and C. Jordan. 1974. *Culture, Behavior and Education.* Beverly Hills, Cal.: Sage.

Goffman, E. 1976. Replies and responses. *Language in Society 5,* 3: 257–313.

Good, T. L. 1979. Teacher effectiveness in the elementary school. *Journal of Teacher Education 30,* 2: 52–64.

Good, T. L., and T. M. Beckerman. 1978. Time on task: a naturalistic study in sixth grade classrooms. *Elementary School Journal 78:* 193–201.

Good, T. L., and J. Brophy. 1973. *Looking in Classrooms.* New York: Harper & Row. (New edition 1987.)

Good, T. L., and S. Marshall. 1984. Do students learn more in heterogeneous or homogeneous groups? In P. Peterson, L. C. Wilkinson, and M. Hallinan (eds.), *The Social Context of Instruction: Group Organization and Group Processes.* New York: Academic Press.

Gore L. 1979. *Listening to Maggie.* London: Longman.

Halliday, M. A. K., and R. Hasan. 1976. *Cohesion in English.* London: Longman.

Harmer, J. 1983. *The Practice of English Language Teaching.* London: Longman.

Hatch, E. 1978. *Second Language Acquisition.* Rowley, Mass.: Newbury House.

Helgesen, M., S. Brown, and T. Mandeville. 1987. *English Firsthand.* Tokyo: Lingual House.

Heuring, D. L. 1984. The revision strategies of skilled and unskilled ESL writers: five case studies. Master's thesis. University of Hawaii at Manoa.

Hieke, A. E. 1981. A content-processing view of hesitation phenomena. *Language and Speech 24,* 2: 147–60.

1985. A componential approach to oral fluency evaluation. *Modern Language Journal 69,* 2: 135–41.

Higgs, T., and R. Clifford. 1982. The push toward communication. In T. Higgs (ed.), *Curriculum, Competence, and the Foreign Language Teacher.* Skokie, Ill.: National Textbook Co.

Hirsch, E. D., Jr. 1977. *The Philosophy of Composition.* Chicago: University of Chicago Press.

Hoey, M. 1979. *Signalling in Discourse: A Functional Analysis of a Common Discourse Pattern in Written and Spoken English.* University of Birmingham: English Language Research Unit.

1983. *On the Surface of Discourse.* London: George Allen & Unwin.

Holden, S. 1981. *Drama in Language Teaching.* London: Longman.

Holmes, V. M. 1984. Sentence planning in a story continuation task. *Language and Speech 27:* 115–34.

Hosenfeld, C. 1977. A preliminary investigation of the reading strategies of successful and non-successful second language learners. *System 5:* 110–23.

1979. A learning-teaching view of second language instruction. *Foreign Language Annals 12*, 1: 51–4.

1984. Case studies of ninth grade readers. In J. C. Alderson and A. H. Urquhart (eds.), *Reading in a Foreign Language*, pp. 231–49. London: Longman.

Hughey, J. B., D. Wormuth, F. Hartfiel, and H. Jacobs. 1983. *Teaching ESL Composition: Principles and Techniques*. Rowley, Mass.: Newbury House.

Hull, J. 1986. *Role Play Activities in Second Language Teaching*. Master's thesis. University of Hawaii.

Hurd, P. D., J. T. Robinson, M. C. McConnell, and N. M. Ross. 1981. *The Status of Middle and High School Science*. Louisville, Col.: Center for Educational Research and Evaluation, BSCS.

Ingram, D. E. 1982. Designing a language program. *RELC Journal 13*, 2: 64–86.

Iwanicki, E. F., and L. McEachern. 1984. Using teacher self-assessment to identify staff development needs. *Journal of Teacher Education 35*, 2: 38–41.

Jarvis, G., and S. Adams. 1979. *Evaluating a Second Language Program*. Washington, D.C.: Center for Applied Linguistics.

Johnson, K. 1982. *Communicative Syllabus Design and Methodology*. Oxford: Pergamon.

Johnson, R. K. 1981. On syllabuses and on being communicative. *The English Bulletin* (Hong Kong) 7, 4: 52–60.

Jones, L. 1983. *Eight Simulations*. Cambridge: Cambridge University Press.

Jones, L., and C. von Baeyer. 1983. *Functions of American English*. New York: Cambridge University Press.

Kantor, K. J. 1984. Classroom contexts and the development of writing intuitions: an ethnographic case study. In R. Beach and L. S. Bridwell (eds.)., *New Directions in Composition Research*, pp. 72–94. New York: Guilford Press.

Keller, E., and Taba-Warner, S. 1976. *Gambits 1*. Ottawa: Supply & Services Canada.

Kelly, L. 1969. *Twenty-five Centuries of Language Teaching*. Rowley, Mass.: Newbury House.

King, M., B. Fagan, T. Bratt, and R. Baer. 1987. ESL and social studies instruction. In Crandall (ed.).

Klippel, F. 1984. *Keep Talking*. Cambridge: Cambridge University Press.

Koch, C., and J. M. Brazil. 1978. *Strategies for Teaching the Composition Process*. Urbana, Ill.: National Council of Teachers of English.

Koziol, S. M., and P. Burns. 1985. Using teacher self-reports for monitoring English instruction. *English Education 17*, 2, 113–120.

Koziol, S. M., and M. E. Call. 1986. Constructing and using teacher self-report inventories. Paper presented at the annual TESOL Convention, Anaheim, March.

Krahnke, K. 1987. *Approaches to Syllabus Design for Foreign Language Teaching*. Englewood Cliffs, N.J.: Prentice-Hall.

Lapp, R. 1984. The process approach to writing: towards a curriculum for international students. Master's thesis. Working Paper available from Department of English as a Second Language, University of Hawaii.

Lee, J. F., and D. Musumeci. 1988. On hierarchies of reading skills and text types. *Modern Language Journal 72*, 2: 173–87.

Lessons from the Vietnamese. 1981. Cambridge: National Extension College.

Lindemann, E. 1982. *A Rhetoric for Writing Teachers.* New York: Oxford University Press.

Liskin-Gasparro, J. E. 1984. The ACTFL proficiency guidelines: a historical perspective. In T. V. Higgs (ed.), *Teaching for Proficiency: the Organizing Principle,* pp. 11–42. Skokie, Ill.: National Textbook Co.

Littlewood, W. 1981. *Communicative Language Teaching.* Cambridge: Cambridge University Press.

Livingstone, C. 1983. *Role Play in Language Learning.* London: Longman.

Long, M., and P. Porter. 1985. Groupwork, interlanguage talk, and second language acquisition. *TESOL Quarterly 19*, 2: 207–28.

Long, M. H. 1983. Process and product in ESL program evaluation. *TESOL Quarterly 18*, 3: 409–25.

Long, M. H., and C. J. Sato. 1983. Classroom foreigner talk discourse: forms and functions of teachers' questions. In Seliger and Long (eds.).

Lougheed, L. 1985. *Listening between the Lines.* Reading, Mass.: Addison-Wesley.

Luft, J. 1969. *Of Human Interaction.* New York: National Press Books.

MacPherson, M., and P. Smith. 1979. *English in Industry: Formulae for Beginners.* Canberra: Australian Government Publishing Services.

Mager, R. F. 1962. *Preparing Instructional Objectives.* Belmont, Cal.: Pitman.

McLaughlin, B. 1985. *Second-Language Acquisition in Childhood,* Vol. 2: *School-Age Children.* 2nd ed. Englewood Cliffs, N.J.: Erlbaum.

McLean, A. 1981. *Start Listening.* London: Longman.

Mohan, B. A. 1986. *Language and Content.* Reading, Mass.: Addison-Wesley.

Moore, D. W., S. A. Moore, P. M. Cunningham, and J. Cunningham. 1986. *Developing Readers and Writers in the Content Areas K–12.* New York: Longman.

Mrowicki, L., R. Jones, and C. Porter. No date. *Project Work English, Competency-Based Curriculum, Level One Survival Curriculum,* Northwest Educational Cooperative, Des Plaines, Ill. Chicago: Illinois Department of Public Aid.

Munby, J. 1978. *Communicative Syllabus Design.* Cambridge: Cambridge University Press.

Murray, D. M. 1980. Writing as process: how writing finds its own meaning. In T. R. Donovan and W. McClelland, *Eight Approaches to the Teaching of Composition,* pp. 3–20. Urbana, Ill.: National Council of Teachers of English.

Naiman, N., M. Fröhlich, H. H. Stern, and A. Todesco. 1978. *The Good Language Learner.* Toronto: Ontario Institute for Studies in Education.

Nunan, D. 1985. Using objective grids in planning language courses. *Prospect 1*, 2: 19–31.

1988. *Syllabus Design.* Oxford: Oxford University Press.

Nuttall, C. 1983. *Teaching Reading Skills in a Foreign Language*. London: Heinemann.

Olson, D. R. 1977. From utterance to text: the bias of language in speech and writing. *Harvard Education Review 47*, 3, 257–81.

Omaggio, A. 1986. *Teaching Language in Context*. Boston: Heinle & Heinle.

Omaggio, A., P. Eddy, L. McKim, and A. Pfannkuche. 1979. Looking at the results. In J. K. Phillips (ed.), *The New Imperative: Expanding the Horizons of Foreign Language Education*. Skokie, Ill.: National Textbook Co.

O'Malley, J., and A. U. Chamot. 1989. *Learner Strategies in Second Language Acquisition*. New York: Cambridge University Press.

O'Malley, J., A. U. Chamot, G. Stewner-Manzanares, R. P. Russo, and L. Kupper. 1985a. Learning strategy applications with students of English as a second language. *TESOL Quarterly 19*, 3: 557–84.

O'Malley, J., A. U. Chamot, G. Stewner-Manzanares, L. Kupper, and R. P. Russo. 1985b. Learning strategies used by beginning and intermediate ESL learners. *Language Learning 35*, 1.

Ongteco, B. C. 1987. Teacher-student interaction patterns in bilingual and mainstream classrooms. Ph.D. dissertation. University of Hawaii at Manoa.

Oxford, R. 1985a. *A New Taxonomy of Second Language Learning Strategies*. Washington, D.C.: Center for Applied Linguistics.

1985b. Second language learning strategies: what the research has to say. *ERIC/CLL News Bulletin 9*, 1.

Pak, J. 1985. *Find Out How You Teach*. Adelaide, Australia: National Curriculum Resource Centre.

Pattison, P. 1987. *Developing Communication Skills*. Cambridge: Cambridge University Press.

Pawley, A., and F. Syder. 1983. Two puzzles for linguistic theory: nativelike selection and nativelike fluency. In J. C. Richards and R. Schmidt (eds.), *Language and Communication*. London: Longman.

Philips, S. V. 1972. Participant structures and communicative competence: Warm Springs Indian children in community classrooms. In C. Cazden, V. John, and D. Hymes (eds.), *Functions of Language in the Classroom*. New York: Teachers College Press.

Phillips, J. 1975. Second language reading: teaching decoding skills. *Foreign Language Annals 8*: 227–30.

Pica, T. 1987. Second-language acquisition, social interaction, and the classroom. *Applied Linguistics 8*, 1:3–21.

Popham, W. J. 1975. *Educational Evaluation*. Englewood Cliffs, N.J.: Prentice-Hall.

Porter, P. 1986. How learners talk to each other: input and interaction in task-centered discussion. In R. Day (ed.), *Talking to Learn: Conversation in Second Language Acquisition*. Rowley, Mass.: Newbury House.

Pratt, D. 1980. *Curriculum Design and Development*. New York: Harcourt Brace Jovanovich.

Proett, J., and K. Gill. 1986. *The Writing Process: A Handbook for Teachers*. Urbana, Ill.: National Council of Teachers of English.

References

Raimes, A. 1983. *Techniques in Teaching Writing.* New York: Oxford University Press.

1985. What unskilled ESL students do as they write: a classroom study of composing. *TESOL Quarterly 19,* 2: 229–59.

Richards, J., and D. Bycina. 1984. *Person to Person.* New York: Oxford University Press.

Richards, J. C. 1985a. Listening comprehension: approach, design, and procedure. In J. C. Richards, *The Context of Language Teaching,* pp. 189–207. New York: Cambridge University Press.

1985b. Conversational competence through role play activities. *RELC Journal 16,* 1: 82–100.

1987. The dilemma of teacher education in TESOL. *TESOL Quarterly 21,* 2: 209–226.

Richards, J. C., D. Gordon, and A. Harper. 1987. *Listen for It.* New York: Oxford University Press.

Richards, J. C., and J. Hull. 1987. *As I Was Saying.* Reading, Mass.: Addison-Wesley.

Richards, J. C., J. Platt, and H. Weber. 1985. *Longman Dictionary of Applied Linguistics.* London: Longman.

Richards, J. C., and T. Rodgers. 1986. *Approaches and Methods in Language Teaching.* New York: Cambridge University Press.

Richards, J. C., and R. Schmidt. 1983. Conversational analysis. In J. C. Richards and R. Schmidt (eds.), *Language and Communication.* London: Longman.

Roberts, C. 1980. Needs analysis for ESL programmes. *Language Learning and Communication 1,* 1: 105–20.

Robinson, P. 1980. *English for Specific Purposes.* Oxford: Pergamon.

Rodgers, T. S. 1986. Changing models of language program evaluation: a case study. Paper presented at the International Conference on Language Program Evaluation, Chulalongkorn University, Bangkok, December.

Rodgers, T. S., and J. C. Richards. 1987. Teacher-based curriculum development: illusion or reality? In J. Burton (ed.), *Implementing the Learner-Centred Curriculum,* pp. 7–43. Adelaide, Australia: National Curriculum Resource Centre.

Rost, M. 1986. *Strategies in Listening.* San Francisco: Lateral Communications.

Rubin, J. 1975. What the good language learner can teach us. *TESOL Quarterly 9,* 1: 41–51.

1981. Study of cognitive processes in second language learning. *Applied Linguistics 11,* 2: 117–31.

Russo, R. P., and G. Stewner-Manzanares. 1985. The training and use of learning strategies for English as a second language in a military context. Paper presented at the annual meeting of the American Educational Research Association, Chicago.

Saville-Troike, M. 1984. What really matters in second language learning for academic achievement? *TESOL Quarterly 18,* 2: 199–220.

Schaffarzick, J., and D. Hampson (eds.). 1975. *Strategies for Curriculum Development.* Berkeley: McCutchan.

Schank, R., and R. P. Abelson. 1977. *Scripts, Plans, Goals and Understanding.* Hillsdale, N. J.: Erlbaum.

Schegloff, E., and H. Sacks. 1973. Opening up closings. *Semiotica 8:* 289–327.

Schinke-Llano, L. 1983. Foreigner talk in content classrooms. In Seliger and Long (eds.), pp. 146–65.

Schmidt, R., and S. Frota. 1986. Developing basic conversational ability in a second language: a case study of an adult learner of Portuguese. In R. Day (ed.), *Talking to Learn: Conversation in Second Language Acquisition.* Rowley, Mass.: Newbury House.

Schroder, K. 1981. Language needs in industry. In R. Freudenstein, J. Beneke, and H. Ponisch (eds.), *Language Incorporated: Teaching Foreign Languages in Industry,* pp. 43–53. Oxford: Pergamon Press.

Seliger, H. W., and M. H. Long (eds.). 1983. *Classroom Oriented Research in Second Language Acquisition.* Rowley, Mass.: Newbury House.

Shaw, A. M. 1977. Foreign language syllabus development: some recent approaches. *Language Teaching and Linguistics: Abstracts 10,* 4: 217–33.

Slade, D. 1986. Teaching casual conversation to adult ESL learners. *Prospect 2,* 1: 68–87.

Stallings, J. A., and D. H. Kaskowitz. 1974. *Follow through Classroom Observation Evaluation, 1972–1973.* Menlo Park, Cal.: Stanford Research Institute.

Stein, B. S., and U. Albridge. 1978. The role of conceptual frameworks in prose comprehension and recall. Mimeo. Vanderbilt University, Nashville.

Stenhouse, L. 1975. *An Introduction to Curriculum Research and Development.* London: Heinemann.

Stern, H. H. 1975. What can we learn from the good language learner? *Canadian Modern Language Review 31:* 304–18.

Swaffar, J. K., K. Arens, and M. Morgan. 1982. Teacher classroom practices: redefining method as task hierarchy. *Modern Language Journal 66,* 1: 24–33.

Syder, F. 1983. *The Fourth R: Spoken Language, English Teaching and Social Competence.* Auckland: Frances Syder.

Taba, H. 1962. *Curriculum Development: Theory and Practice.* New York: Harcourt Brace.

Teruya, A., and J. Wong. 1972. *The Filipino Immigrant Child: Handbook for Teachers.* Honolulu: University of Hawaii.

Tikunoff, W. J. 1983. Utility of the SBIF features for the instruction of limited English proficient students. Report No. SBIF-83-R.15/16 for NIE Contract No. 400-80-0026. San Francisco: Far West Laboratory for Educational Research and Development.

    1985. *Applying Significant Bilingual Instructional Features in the Classroom.* Rosslyn, Va.: National Clearinghouse for Bilingual Education.

Tikunoff, W. J., B. A. Ward, C. A. Fisher, J. C. Armendariz, L. Parker, V. J. A. Dominguez, C. Mercado, M. Romero, and T. A. Good. 1980. Review of the literature for a descriptive study of significant bilingual instructional features. Report No. SBIF-81-D.1.1. San Francisco: Far West Laboratory for Educational Research and Development.

University of the State of New York. 1983. *The New York State Core Curriculum for English as a Second Language in the Secondary Schools.* Albany, N.Y.: Bureau of Bilingual Education.

Ur, P. 1981. *Discussions That Work*. Cambridge: Cambridge University Press.

Van Ek, J., and L. Alexander. 1980. *Threshold Level English*. Oxford: Pergamon.

Van Ek, J. A. 1977. *The Threshold Level for Modern Language Learning in Schools*. London: Longman. (Originally published 1976 by the Council of Europe, Strasbourg.)

Van Lier, L. 1988. *The Classroom and the Language Learner*. London: Longman.

Wardhaugh, R. 1985. *How Conversation Works*. Oxford: Blackwell.

Webb, N. M. 1980. A process-outcome of learning in group and individual settings. *Educational Psychologist 15:* 69–83.

Wenden, A. 1983. A literature review: the process of intervention. *Language Learning 33*, 1: 103–21.

1985. Learner strategies. *TESOL Newsletter* (October).

Whitlock, R. 1984. Six writing exercises for helping students understand process. Manuscript. University of Hawaii.

Wilkins, D. A. 1976. *Notional Syllabuses*. Oxford: Oxford University Press.

Willing, K. 1985. *Helping Adults Develop Their Learning Strategies*. Sydney: Adult Migrant Education Service.

1987. Learner strategies as information management. *Prospect 2*, 3: 273–92.

Willis, J. 1981. *Teaching English through English*. London: Longman.

Winskowski, C. 1977. Topicalization work in telephone conversations. *International Journal of Psycholinguistics 4*, 1: 77–93.

1978. A study of the development of topical behavior within an experimental relationship frame. Ph.D. dissertation. University of Hawaii.

Wong Fillmore, L. 1982. Language minority students and school participation: what kind of schooling is needed. *Journal of Education 164*: 143–56.

Worthen, B. R., and J. R. Sanders. 1973. *Educational Evaluation: Theory and Practice*. Columbus, Oh.: Jones Publishing Co.

Yalden, J. 1983. *The Communicative Syllabus: Evolution, Design and Implementation*. Oxford: Pergamon.

Zamel, V. 1987. Recent research on writing pedagogy. *TESOL Quarterly 21*, 4: 697–716.

Zeichner, K. M. 1982. Reflective teaching and field-based experience in teacher education. *Interchange 12*, 4: 1–22.

Zuck, J., and L. Zuck. 1984. Scripts: an example from newspaper texts. *Reading in a Foreign Language 2*, 1: 147–55.

Index

Page numbers in italics indicate material in tables and examples.